Introducing English as an Additional Language to Young Children

Introducing English as an Additional Language to Young Children

A Practical Handbook

Kay Crosse

P·C·P

Paul Chapman
Publishing

Paul Chapman Publishing
A SAGE Publications Ltd
1 Oliver's Yard
55 City Road
London EC1Y 1SP

SAGE Publications Inc.
2455 Teller Road
Thousand Oaks, California 91320

SAGE Publications India Pvt Ltd
B 1/I 1 Mohan Cooperative Industrial Area
Mathura Road, New Delhi 110 044
India

SAGE Publications Asia-Pacific Pte Ltd
33 Pekin Street #02-01
Far East Square
Singapore 048763

Library of Congress Control Number: 2007927738

British Library Cataloguing in Publication Data

A catalogue record for this book is available from the British Library

ISBN 978-1-4129-3610-1
ISBN 978-1-4129-3611-8 (pbk)

Typeset by C&M Digitals (P) Ltd, Chennai, India
Printed in Great Britain by The Cromwell Press, Trowbridge, Wiltshire
Printed on paper from sustainable resources

This book is dedicated with love to Charlotte who continues to sustain my interest in language development through our many memorable and utterly enjoyable conversations and the countless stories that we share together.

And a woman who held a babe against her bosom said, Speak to us of Children.

And he said:

Your children are not your children.

They are the sons and daughters of Life's longing for itself.

They come through you but not from you,

And though they are with you yet they belong not to you.

The Prophet, Kahlil Gibran

(The above extract is from *The Prophet* originally published by William Heinemann Ltd.)

Contents

About the Author

Kay Crosse qualified as a teacher in 1967 and currently works as a supply teacher in Reception and Foundation Stage classes. She lectured in Early Years education and took on other management responsibilities at Norland College over a period of 21 years, in the last 5 years as Principal of the College. Currently Kay works as an Early Years consultant both in the UK and Japan. She was appointed by the Open University and the National Day Nursery Association as a mentor to graduates undertaking the Early Years Professional Status qualifications. She is a Lecturer for the Open University on Early Years courses leading to the award of a Foundation Degree. She was appointed by the National Children's Bureau to work with Early Years professionals in using the Parents and Early Years Learning (PEAL) materials to support parents and their children's learning. She is in involved in writing courses to support training in Early Years education, literacy and numeracy and schema development for young children.

Topic web : Use this chart to plan additional activities connected with an area of learning or a specific theme

	Chapter 6 Personal, social, emotional development	Chapter 7 Communication, language and literacy	Chapter 8 Problem solving, reasoning and numeracy	Chapter 9 Knowledge and understanding of the world	Chapter 10 Physical development	Chapter 11 Creative development
About me	My family My day at nursery My home See what I can do Feelings Keeping safe	When's my birthday? What's the weather like today?	Best foot forward!	Let's celebrate! Where's my nursery? Keeping warm	'A busy, busy, week' Look what I can do	All my own work! Welcome!
Colour	People who help us Keeping safe	When's my birthday?	Dizzy dinosaurs Best foot forward! Who lives in this house?	Keeping warm	Five of the best Toot, toot	All my own work! Mix it up! Working together Let's investigate
Creative activities	All about me People who help us	When's my birthday? Seasons 'Room on the broom' Action rhymes	Dizzy dinosaurs Who lives in this house?	Growing sunflowers Flutter by, butterfly Minibeasts Spiders Let's celebrate! Keeping warm	A busy, busy week Five of the best Let's explore Look what I can do	All my own work! Trip, trap. Trip, trap Welcome! Mix it up! Working together Let's investigate!
ICT	Keeping safe	My favourite story	1, 2, 3 – What's in that tree? *Three Billy Goats Gruff*	Minibeasts Spiders My favourite weather Let's celebrate!	'A busy, busy week'	All my own work!
Mathematical language	Keeping safe	When's my birthday? Seasons Action rhymes Traditional nursery tales	Goldilocks's picnic 1, 2, 3 – What's in that tree? *Three Billy Goats Gruff* Busy bikes Dizzy dinosaurs Best foot forward! Who lives in this house?	Flutter by, butterfly	'A busy, busy week'	Mix it up!

Topic web (Continued)

Measures	See what I can do	My favourite story Action rhymes Traditional nursery rhymes	Busy Bikes Best foot forward!	Growing sunflowers	Toot, toot	Mix it up!
Movement	See what I can do	Days of the week My favourite story Action rhymes	Flippity flop! Busy bikes	My favourite weather	Penguins 'A busy, busy week' Let's explore Look what I can do Toot, toot	Trip, trap. Trip, trap
My nursery	My day at nursery Keeping safe		Busy Bikes	Where's my nursery?	Toot, toot	Welcome!
Natural world	Keeping safe	What's the weather like today?	1, 2, 3 – What's in that tree?	Growing sunflowers Flutter by, butterfly Minibeasts Spiders My favourite weather Where's my nursery? Keeping warm	Penguins Five of the best Let's explore	All my own work! Let's investigate!
Number	All about me My home	Days of the week When's my birthday? Seasons My favourite story	Goldilocks's picnic 1, 2, 3 – What's in that tree? Busy bikes Dizzy dinosaurs Best foot forward! Flippity flop!	Flutter by, butterfly Minibeasts Let's celebrate	Toot, toot	Trip, trap. Trip, trap
Positional language	People who help us My family	When's my birthday?	*Three Billy Goats Gruff* Dizzy dinosaurs Best foot forward! Goldilocks's picnic Who lives in this house?	Minibeasts Spiders	Five of the best	Mix it up!
Rhyming activities	All about me	'Room on the broom' My favourite story	Dizzy dinosaurs Flippity flop!	Spiders My favourite weather	Penguins 'A busy, busy week' Toot, toot	Trip, trap. Trip, trap Working together

(Continued)

Topic web (Continued)

Recording information	My family Feelings Keeping safe	Seasons	1, 2, 3 – What's in that tree? Dizzy dinosaurs	Growing sunflowers Flutter by, butterfly Minibeasts	Five of the best	Welcome!
Role play	My home People who help us Keeping safe	'Room on the broom' Traditional nursery tales	Goldilocks's picnic Best foot forward!	Flutter by, butterfly Let's celebrate Where's my nursery?	Let's explore Toot, toot	Welcome!
Sequencing	My day at nursery	Days of the week When's my birthday? Seasons 'Room on the broom' My favourite story Traditional nursery tales	Goldilocks's picnic *Three Billy Goats Gruff*	Growing sunflowers Minibeasts Flutter by, butterfly	'A busy, busy week'	Trip, trap. Trip, trap
Shape and pattern	My home	When's my birthday What's the weather like today? Seasons	Goldilocks's picnic *Three Billy Goats Gruff* Dizzy dinosaurs Best foot forward! Who lives in this house?	Flutter by, butterfly	Five of the best	All my own work! Welcome! Working together
Stories and rhymes	All about me My family See what I can do Feelings People who help us	Days of the week What's the weather like today? 'Room on the broom' My favourite story Action rhymes Traditional nursery tales	Goldilocks's picnic *Three Billy Goats Gruff* Best foot forward! Dizzy dinosaurs Who lives in this house?	Flutter by, butterfly Spiders My favourite weather Keeping warm	Let's explore Look what I can do	Trip, trap. Trip, trap My favourite weather Welcome!

Introduction

This book is for all early years practitioners working with young children in nursery schools, pre-schools and day nurseries together with childminders and nannies working as home-based child carers. The focus of the book is to offer activities and guidance for practitioners working with children learning English as an additional language. However, the approach described and the practical activities included will work well with all children who need support to improve their confidence and language skills. The development and use of communication and language are at the heart of all children's learning and the way in which young children are able to experience and become involved in stories, rhymes, music, poetry and language will affect their progress and enjoyment in all areas of the early years curriculum. This is an exciting time to be working in the early years. Practitioners are keen to develop their skills and knowledge and to gain higher levels of qualifications such as an Early Childhood degree, a Foundation degree or the Early Years Professional status. The higher the qualification of the adult working with young children, the better quality of teaching they are likely to have.

The survey carried out in 2005 by the National Centre for Languages, 'Positively Pluringual', reminds us of the linguistic, educational and intellectual resources that children and their families using community languages bring to early years settings. The survey reflects the current situation:

> Our society is changing, and our need for good communication across cultures has never been greater. The UK has a major linguistic asset in its multicultural population which, if developed wisely and inclusively alongside English and other languages, has the potential to benefit society as a whole as well as improving the life chances of individual children. (2005: 4)

Many children are multilingual and are learning two or three languages including English with different members of their families and may also use a different language in religious contexts.

In September 2005 the *Times Educational Supplement* published an article by Carline Roberts indicating that there were around 700,000 children in the United Kingdom who had a language other than English as their first language – this was more than 10 per cent of the school population. In the same article references were made to the paucity of training and support for teachers who have the responsibility of supporting children learning English as an additional language.

Children who are learning English as an additional language come from a wide variety of backgrounds including:

- children born in Britain but who do not start to learn English until they start at an early years setting or formal schooling

- children who are brought up bilingually and are learning English as well as their first or home language

- children who are newly arrived in England and are fluent in their home or first language and may have a knowledge of English as a foreign language

- children who are new arrivals and are fluent in their home or first language and have a little knowledge of some everyday English

- children who are new arrivals and have no previous experience of English and have very basic literacy skills in their home or first language.

The work that is carried out in early years settings, to welcome children and their families and to promote their home language and culture while building English language skills, will influence attitudes to education for a lifetime. Central to this book are issues of equality, diversity and inclusion. Where there is effective, inclusive practice children who are new to the English language as well as children with disabilities or with additional learning needs are able to access the early years curriculum and reach their full potential. Children from minority religious, ethnic and cultural groups can contribute a wealth of experiences and knowledge to benefit all the children attending the setting.

The introduction of the Every Child Matters agenda sets out the framework for professional staff working in a wide range of services for children to come together to work in ways that reduce disadvantage and enable all children to benefit from their early years care and education. The five key aspects of Every Child Matters will be central to the Early Years Foundation Stage due to be implemented in 2008.

The Childcare Act 2006 takes forward the key commitments from the 10-year *Childcare Strategy* published in 2004 and places on local authorities and their partners the responsibility to improve the outcomes for all children up to age 5 and to reduce inequalities within the Every Child Matters framework. The Childcare Act 2006 also provides the underpinning legislation for the single framework of the Early Years Foundation Stage which supports practitioners in developing children's care, learning and development from birth to the end of the school Reception year. The Early Years Foundation Stage brings together the *Birth to Three Matters* framework, the *Curriculum Guidance for the Foundation Stage* and the National Standards for under-8s' day care and childminding. This single framework is planned to be a statutory requirement in 2008. However, many settings have made the decision to implement the new framework before this date.

The book is organised into two parts. The first provides underpinning knowledge that enables the practitioner to understand ways in which their knowledge of child development will enable them to plan effectively to meet the individual needs of children. Practitioners who know why they do what they do and who can articulate this effectively can successfully explain the importance of play and first-hand experiences for children who are developing their language skills. Where play is central to language learning, children are able to learn their new language in a context which is meaningful to them. As they develop their role play there is a purpose in trying out their new language skills and a delight in being able to communicate successfully with an increasing number of children and adults in their setting. The context is the key to progress and this book offers a range of contexts for children to learn, practise and consolidate their language skills. The importance of promoting personal, emotional and social development is discussed together with ways in which this affects all other areas of development. The first part of the book, Chapters 1 to 5, identifies ways in which children can learn best in a nurturing environment together with the importance of the practitioner developing their reflective skills and taking part in other professional development activity.

The second part of the book, Chapters 6 to 11, is organised using the six areas of learning forming the Early Years Foundation Stage curriculum. Each of the areas of learning has suggested practical activities which will promote language learning, together with the way in which the activity can be organised and the resources which are necessary. Although this is a helpful way of organising the activities, it is important to remember that each of the activities will promote many areas of development and be relevant to more than one curriculum area of learning. A topic web (pp. x–xii) is included for practitioners to cross-reference each of the activities and to know where further ideas are available to develop one particular theme such as counting or to further develop a particular skill such as promoting ICT skills.

The two parts of the book are interrelated as effective practitioners use their knowledge and understanding to underpin their practice. This approach is based on the Froebel principle of closely linking theory and practice. It mirrors the approach used in this book where the starting point is what children already know and then staff build on this knowledge in ways that children can make connections in their learning and progress with confidence and, in so doing, raise their self-esteem. This is particularly important for children who are learning English as an additional language and who may be adjusting to living in a different country and attending an early years setting for the first time. Each of the activities in the second part contains information about how to carry out the activity together with ways of extending this activity. Ideally the activities are carried out with a small group of children, but not necessarily only with children new to English. The activities are those which will form part of the early years curriculum for all children but there is benefit from having a special language focus and of being aware of the needs of a particular group of children. Each of the activities may well need to be undertaken over a sustained period of time and should not be viewed as a one-hour or one session's activity. Children need to time to develop their play and consolidate their skills, to reflect on their experiences and become autonomous learners. Sometimes they want to change or add to their previous work and skilled practitioners are able to adjust their planning to accommodate the children's ideas and perhaps head off into new directions for learning. Practitioners are always able to learn and continue their professional development if time is taken to observe and listen to the children. This is part of what makes working with young children so exciting and enjoyable!

Foundations of language learning

This chapter considers the following aspects of children starting to learn English as an additional language:

- Language, culture and learning
- Child development
- Foundations for oral language skills
- Working with parents to provide consistency and security for young children
- Support for parents
- Building relationships
- The role of the adult in supporting children's language learning
- Using the child's first language in school and at home
- An overview of the Early Years Foundation Stage curriculum.

Language, culture and learning

Many early years settings now welcome children and families from different cultures who use languages other than English. Young children who are starting to learn English as an additional language may also be attending a nursery school, pre-school, day nursery or childminder perhaps for the first time. They will bring with them many skills and experiences from their home culture and will be both anxious and excited about their new situation. A good foundation for learning English as an additional language is embedded in quality early years practice. Good early years practice is based on the following principles:

- Equality of opportunity which enables all children to reach their full potential.

- Valuing play as an enjoyable and challenging activity.

- Emphasising and building on what children can do rather than what they cannot do.

- An understanding of child development leading to appropriate activities for children.

- Giving priority to personal, social and emotional development.

- Encouraging children to become independent, autonomous learners.

- Learning based on first-hand experiences which is then evaluated.

- Effective record-keeping and assessment identifying what children learn and how they learn.

- Highly qualified staff working in partnership with parents and carers.

- Staff who are reflective and analytical practitioners.

The ways in which children learn best through play and first-hand experiences are also the most appropriate ways for them to become either bilingual or multilingual. The nature of bilingualism for young children can be very varied. It can be an additional language used by them at nursery while they use their first language with their parents, grandparents and within their local community. In some families each parent may have a different language and the child is learning these languages from birth and then English at school. Some of these children may be newly arrived in England. Children are skilled at switching between languages and can become proficient and accomplished bilingual or multilingual speakers. For this to happen, however, they need to be supported in their first language and culture, and to be helped to settle happily into their new environment. Children as young as two can quickly learn which language is used in which circumstance and can switch from one language to another. Their progress in each language can initially be slower as they grapple with different vocabulary and sentence structures but their language development catches up with their monolingual peers by the age of five or six. Children who are bilingual seem to have more awareness of how language works and an increased sensitivity to language use. They listen carefully and use the full range of communication methods to make themselves understood and also to understand. Younger children are less inhibited than older children and once they feel comfortable in their new surroundings they will join in wholeheartedly with activities, contributing in as many ways as possible and eventually joining in and developing their language skills.

An appreciation of the diverse experiences and cultures that the children bring with them into the nursery can be through music, art and dance as well as stories, rhymes and poems. These provide a rich treasure chest on which new English language skills can be built as well as a huge amount of resource material which can be shared with all members of the class – children and staff. As children increase their English language skills, they become more confident in sharing aspects of their home culture, learning about their new culture and gradually finding it easier to join in with all of the play and activities associated with the English Early Years Foundation Stage curriculum.

Providing support for children

There are now many ways of supporting children in early years settings, through staff employed as bilingual teaching assistants, bilingual nursery nurses and teachers who may be based in one particular setting or travel to several settings during one week sharing their expertise with more children and families. They act as interpreters as well as supporting the children's 'settling in period' and the classroom activities. In many localities there are specific services that can also support staff and children. The first priority of all staff working in bilingual settings is to help the child and the child's family feel welcome and at ease in their new environment. It is helpful if staff know some of the important words from the child's first language and some of the customs of their first culture. This knowledge helps staff to understand more about the child and to smooth the way for the child becoming part of the peer group. By valuing the home language and culture, first language skills are developed properly and, in time, the additional language is also developed. Think about how children gain their first language through listening to parents and other children, by joining in songs during routine daily events, by repetition of enjoyable and fun rhymes and sharing stories. This is the ideal way to learn an additional language.

Marie enjoyed the times when her father read her the book *I won't bite* by Rod Campbell, translated by Haan Associates. They had borrowed the English/Somali dual language version from the local library. Marie particularly enjoyed the sensory aspects of this touch and feel book, stroking the mouse's ear, the rabbit's fluffy tail and the chimp's furry chest! She pretended to be very scared and hid behind her hands at the end of the book when she saw the enormous teeth of the crocodile. She soon learnt the much repeated phrase 'I won't bite' in both Somali and English.

Developing a sense of belonging

All children need to grow up knowing that they belong. A sense of belonging provides a way of constructing identity and of knowing who you are and where you belong. Children can feel a sense of belonging to their immediate and extended family, to their community and to their nursery setting. Their sense of culture can be strengthened through contact with all these groups. Children are more likely to feel a sense of belonging when the language they use and the customs they and their family observe are respected.

Child development

When adults working with young children have a thorough understanding of all aspects of child development, they are able to plan activities effectively, which promote the all-round development of young children. Play is at the heart of young children's learning and offers a wealth of opportunities for emerging bilingual children to develop both first and additional language skills. Although each aspect of development – physical development, cognitive and language development, emotional and social development and spiritual development – may be approached for planning purposes as separate entities, it is essential to view development in young children from a holistic standpoint. In this way the children make connections in their play, their learning and their daily experiences. When development is seen holistically, the child is then at the centre of the planning and their differing needs can be met. Learning (cognitive development) cannot take place unless the child is happy and settled in their new environment (emotional, social and spiritual development) and healthy (physical development).

Maslow's (1908–70) 'Hierarchy of Needs' theory is a generally regarded as useful way of thinking about children's and adults' needs. The needs identified at a lower level such as safety, security and nutrition must be met before needs at a higher level, such as self-esteem and cognitive development, can be promoted.

Physical development

When children are involved in play activities they are developing both their fine-motor skills and their large-motor skills. Fine-motor skills involve small movements such as threading and drawing. Children practise large-motor skills when running, hopping, jumping and using tricycles. As they delight in playing games such as hopscotch there are opportunities to learn and practise counting in several languages. This is a natural way of learning to count, which then can be practised in other situations such as building a tower and counting the bricks. The skilled practitioner uses routine everyday activities within the nursery, looking for the language opportunities within. When the children get ready to play outside, this involves them putting on hats and coats which encourages independence and gives them practice with fine-motor skills. However, this also gives them the opportunity to hear new vocabulary such as 'hat', 'bobble hat', 'red bobble hat' or 'bright blue cap'. The adult scaffolds or builds up the language in an appropriate context.

Cognitive development

Learning is an interactive process planned to include both adult- and child-led activities as well as responding to unplanned spontaneous learning opportunities. When children are interested in their learning and the task matches their level of understanding, they are motivated to learn. Children who are learning a second language need to have the task set at an appropriate level for their stage of intellectual development as well as encouraging their additional language skills. They may need support and guidance at the start of the task but can then work independently alongside their peer group. Their cognitive ability may be initially above that of their English language ability but staff need to make every effort to offer meaningful activities.

Planning for cognitive or intellectual development involves many aspects of the learning process:

- problem solving

- developing and understanding concepts

- developing creativity and imagination

- concentration

- memory

- acquiring knowledge and new experiences

- learning through play.

Language development

Language development encompasses both spoken and written language. Spoken language forms the basis of all language and literacy development, and the more early involvement with songs, stories, poems and rhymes that young children have, the easier it will be to acquire reading and writing skills at a later stage. Sensory play provides many language opportunities – think of the vocabulary that can emerge from cornflour and jelly play! Staff who plan language-based activities and who sensitively model the appropriate language will find that young children 'pick up' the language and in time use the same language in other contexts. Just as in the children's first language, bilingual children will understand the language long before speaking it. Bilingual children will acquire their new language in a similar sequence to their first language. There is often a silent period when children are taking in the new vocabulary and sentence structures, followed by early attempts with two- or three-word combinations. There is frequently a stage where vocabulary from both languages is used as children make great efforts to communicate using whatever tools are at their disposal – much like adults on holiday in a foreign country! In these early attempts at communication it is vital that children are supported in their efforts and receive praise and encouragement to spur them on to greater efforts.

Social and emotional development

The promotion of both social and emotional development is closely linked in young children. For learning to take place, young children have to feel socially and emotionally at ease. To make those first tentative steps in their new language they have to feel secure and know that they are learning in a supportive environment. The time spent by staff in helping children and their families feel welcome will provide a sense of belonging. The social and emotional development of young children has to be the first priority of staff. A sense of being included in their new setting from the very first moment is of enormous importance to a young child. Practical steps such as making sure the child has a place at circle time and has an identifiable coat-peg translate into a feeling of belonging. The use of the visual timetable helps children to know and anticipate daily activities. Skilled practitioners ensure that the child is supported into group activities, especially in informal activities such as playtime and lunch time. Some children naturally empathise with children new to the setting and can act as sensitive guides or buddies shepherding the new children through seemingly challenging situations. Being part of a group where other children act as good language models is a helpful learning environment. In this way children will build on their existing social skills and will share, co-operate, build confidence and generally enjoy making new friends. Informal observation by staff at these crucial times is essential. How else will staff know that children are happy and ready to learn?

As children develop their social skills they build relationships and sound emotional foundations. Self-esteem and self-worth are at the heart of all learning and this includes learning an additional language. When a child knows that their home culture, languages, skills and knowledge are valued, they have the foundations for future success. Praise, encouragement and support are evidence to the child that all these aspects are thought of as important. This is essential not only for the child who is acquiring new language skills, but also for all the children in the class. If staff recognise that the child is playing and learning in a totally new environment as well as learning new language concepts, then there is an understanding of why the child may appear reluctant to join in with activities and initially may observe rather than participate.

Spiritual development

This aspect of children's all-round development is sometimes neglected. It is connected with developing and building on very young children's sense of wonder and appreciation, their sense of self in connection with the universe and, in later years, developing a sense of fairness and knowing right from wrong. As adults we are becoming more aware of our responsibility with regard to environmental issues and to children and their families living in other parts of the world. Young children can learn about these issues in ways relevant to them, especially through first-hand experiences. From the age of three years children are beginning to look outwards and to be interested in other children and their possibly different views. Children who are learning English as an additional language have the opportunity to learn vocabulary connected with feelings and this can be helpful to them when trying to express their views about their new situation. It can take some time for emerging bilingual children to be able to articulate their feelings, and staff need to be very observant when assessing a child's well-being.

Foundations for oral language skills

Oral language skills are key factors for children in developing literacy skills. Young children use similar strategies in acquiring their additional languages to those they do in their first language. Concepts built in the children's first language transfer over time to their additional language. Parents have great success as their child's first language teachers and can be encouraged to support their child's efforts in acquiring another language. Children need a wealth of oral language skills which a good early years setting will offer. There are frequent opportunities in play activities for children to learn vocabulary and phrases in the play context and then, after a period of consolidation, to use their newly acquired knowledge in different contexts. The context for language learning is very important as it offers children some clues as to meaning, and the play context provides a purpose for them to develop and practise their skills. The importance of context in helping children to acquire language skills cannot be overemphasised.

Good listening skills enable children quickly to respond to their new language. It is beneficial not only to have the ability to listen carefully, but also to discriminate between sounds. Young children will be exposed to many noises as part of every day life and they may need practise in tuning in to specific sounds such as the beginning and ending of words. Even more important is the attitude towards taking 'risks' and trying out those first few words in a new environment. On these occasions a positive response from parents and staff is essential. When 'mistakes' are inevitably made, a simple, low key correction in the form of modelling the right word or phrase is helpful. This is the way in which parents help their children learning their first language.

Learning language through play

Block play is a useful example of ways in which not only oral language is promoted but also all aspects of development. As a creative group activity there are plenty of opportunities for children of all languages and abilities to play together and to use their creative and engineering skills. Through block play children's development is promoted holistically and all aspects of development benefit in the following ways.

Physical development – using fine manipulative skills to place and move the blocks.

Cognitive development – decision-making and problem solving.

Language development – language involving participating, sharing, co-operating and sharing.

Social development – playing alongside and with other children. Leading and following.

Emotional development – receiving praise and encouragement. Satisfaction and pride.

Spiritual development – developing concepts of helpfulness and fairness.

It is beneficial for staff to plan particular language strategies for activities such as block play. Staff can model ways in which the developing bilingual child can ask to join in with the activity. If there is a need to introduce and practise the use of positional vocabulary such as 'on top of', 'behind', 'in front of', 'in the middle of', then sensitive adult involvement in block play is a useful strategy. Children hear the phrase and then see the action of placing the blocks and make a natural connection between the two. Repetition is needed for that phrase or phrases to become part of the child's vocabulary. In this way there is a context for learning and it has far more meaning for the child than learning the same words as part of a vocabulary list.

Working with parents to provide consistency and security for young children

All children benefit when their carers and educators work closely with parents. Children sense the warm support when their key worker and parents talk together about progress, share the enjoyment of a child's learning and enjoy the humorous moments that occur in nursery life. The first contact between home and school may be the initial enquiry or admission visit. Ideally, this first contact should be a very positive experience for the family and child. However, this can be difficult from a language standpoint if there is no one available who can speak the parents' home language. In nurseries and schools where there may be frequent enquiries from non-English-speaking families some groundwork in the community will be useful. When families know that an interpreter for a particular language is present in a school on a regular day each week and that an initial enquiry on a particular day of the week enables the interpreter to help the family, they may choose to use this facility and visit the school on that particular day. Local authority language support groups can also help if the setting has prior knowledge of the language requirements.

An interpreter will be particularly beneficial during any home visit and should have an appreciation of the home–school partnership and an understanding of the activities of the early years setting. Parents may be more relaxed and communicative with the support of an interpreter when the visit takes place in the parents' home environment. This visit should not just become a forum of extracting information from the parents about their child but more a two-way exchange of knowledge – the parents' knowledge about their culture and their child, and knowledge offered to the parents about the way in which the setting functions and the way in which their new culture works. A video, a DVD or collection of photographs which accurately depict a normal day will be helpful for parents. It is useful if parents are helped to have a realistic understanding of the way in which their child will learn an additional language, including the facts that initial progress may appear to be slow, the first language will be spoken and valued, and that it takes many years to become fluent. Many parents, not only those coming to the UK from other countries, view time spent by young children in playing as non-productive in a learning sense. The home visit is a time when a brief explanation of how children learn through play and the importance of play in developing their English language can be made. This explanation needs to be further developed as the relationship between home and school is strengthened. Additional information besides the usual name and date of birth, medical information and so on gained through the home visit or the admission visit at school can include:

- country of birth

- languages spoken and understood

- languages written and read

- languages used at home

- which language is used with which parent, sibling or relative

- settings previously attended with and without a parent

- the special interests of the child

- favourite books, nursery rhymes and songs in any language

- special words or customs which will help the child to settle in happily

- special requirements with regard to religious and cultural activities

- the particular concerns of the parents

- lunch arrangements

- arrangements for bringing and collecting the child

- name of a contact who could act as an interpreter.

It is worth taking the time between the home visit or admission visit to organise support for the family and child. This may mean contacting previous settings or arranging for an interpreter to be present in school for the first few days of the child's settling-in period. It is preferable when there is a permanent member of staff to act in a support and interpreting role, but where this is not possible other arrangements need to be made. There should not be too much of an interval between the home visit and the child's first session, which may be with parental support according to the setting policy, and should be fairly short.

Support for parents

Each contact with parents is an opportunity for staff to form a judgement as to how much support will be needed for a parent in the initial stages of being welcomed to the setting. This will depend on many aspects including the parents' English language ability and their understanding of the culture and educational system. The website www.parentcentre.gov.uk offers information to parents about the English education system and ideas as to how to support their children's learning. This information can be downloaded in 11 languages in addition to English. A parent newly arrived in England with their first child starting at school is likely to require consistent and continued support. Some parents can feel quite isolated and at a loss to understand what happens in a setting and what the expectations are of themselves and their child. Information as to how to support parents can be found on www.familyandparenting.org. Support can also come from bilingual nursery staff or from a parent who has had prolonged contact with the school. However, some parents may feel intimidated at the thought of attending a parents' meeting or open day and thought needs to be given to ways of welcoming the less confident parent. This may include having events for the local community where visitors are welcome to 'drop in' and there is no requirement for participation other than through observing the activities.

Where parents are viewed as partners in the learning process and efforts are made to enable each parent who chooses to contribute in an appropriate way, then parents feel valued and part of the setting's community. They understand that the school and the community can work together for the benefit of everybody. Parents, grandparents and other people in the community can offer a wealth of information and expertise relating to the cultures represented in the setting. They often have hidden talents and skills that just need encouraging out into the open to share and to be acknowledged. When the home culture contributes to the children's learning experience, the children gain in self-esteem, skills and knowledge. Schools need policies to support the ways in which parental help is organised, and most schools find that some training for those working in the classroom is beneficial for the teacher and the parent. Settings which do not have staff speaking the family home language can use the online support to be found at www.dgteaz.org.uk. This is the website for Dingle, Granby, Toxteth and City of Liverpool partnership where various letters to parents are available in 32 languages, including Chinese, Croatian, Farsi and French. The letters cover useful topics such as telling parents about trips and visits, and a welcome letter. Another very helpful website is that of the Portsmouth Ethnic Minority Achievement Service which offers guidance to working in partnership with parents as well as working to reduce underachievement in minority ethnic pupils, including those learning English as an additional language – www.blss.portsmouth.sch.uk.

Building relationships

Young bilingual children bring to their new setting a wealth of experiences and language skills connected with their first language and culture. In time, when their language skills are sufficiently developed in their additional language(s) to understand new concepts and ideas, they will be able to transfer the knowledge gained in their first language to their second. They will have a range of skills that they can use confidently to play with other children, make friends and generally cope well with a range of social situations. However, when they first go to their new setting they may, understandably, be anxious with a sense of feeling unable to do many things that the other children can do. A feeling of being different may also add to their worries. These are difficult topics to discuss particularly for settings which do not have the use of an interpreter. Stories are useful ways of raising these issues and of helping all the children in the setting to think about and manage these situations. The *Rainbow Fish* stories by Marcus Pfister deal with difference and isolation. In one of the stories about Rainbow Fish the main character, Rainbow Fish, happily plays 'flash tag' with his friends. One fish does not have a shiny scale and is, therefore, unable to play the game. After some exciting adventures Rainbow Fish welcomes the new fish and changes the game to one of 'fin tag' which then enables all the fish to play. The pictures beautifully illustrate the differences between the fish, and the children do not need an exact understanding of the language to gain an appreciation of the meaning behind the story. There are also other ways to welcome and help a child to settle:

- welcome signs for the child and family in their home language

- clear visual signs to important places in the school or nursery

- using a visual timetable to signal important events such as lunch time and home time

- providing a supportive structure for playtimes and lunch times so that the child is not left alone

- encouraging one of the other children to act as a buddy

- using pictures and other visual aids to support early learning

- giving the child appropriate responsibility for tasks within the group

- allowing time for the child to watch the other children and then to make a response in the way that is most appropriate for the child.

As with all children, effective communication between home and school will help the settling-in process to be achieved in a shorter time. This communication should not be one way as it is essential for the setting to receive feedback from parents about what the child is enjoying and what is still causing anxiety. In these early stages there are bound to be activities that give pleasure and enable the child to make progress in learning and other activities that cause frustration, and the reasons for this need to be explored.

The role of the adult in supporting children's language and learning

In these early stages the most effective means of helping the child to settle is to ensure that the child has a key worker who smoothes the transition for the child from home to school or from one setting to another. Ideally, the key worker will understand the child's home language as well as English. Even if this is not possible, a key worker who is sensitive to the child's new situation can be very effective. The priority is to ensure a safe and reassuring environment in which to learn and to encourage communication by the child in as many ways as they find possible. This safe environment is not only physically safe, but also one in which the child knows that learning risks can be taken and a new language tried and when mistakes are made these are taken as a welcome sign that the child is happy, enthusiastic and keen to attempt new things in their learning. Small-group work where the new child feels nurtured is a good learning environment where the child can either watch and learn or make a contribution to the learning by joining in with the play in small ways. The website developed by Birmingham, Leeds and Manchester local education authorities (LEAs) and funded by the Department for Education and Skills (DfES) offers a range of bilingual resources in addition to information about professional development activities and a newsletter – www.emaonline.org.uk.

The key person is instrumental in making observations at various times and sharing these with all staff. The key worker must be a person who is able to be a good listener and to work effectively with parents, having a sensitivity and understanding of the best ways of supporting children's language learning. All the adults in the early years team need to work together to know that the child is ready to learn. Staff can support the child by:

- facing the child when speaking

- speaking slowly and clearly

- giving the child time to work out what is being said

- using different types of communication including gestures

- using pictures and other visual material when appropriate

- looking for responses other than verbal ones

- understanding that it takes time to speak English but learning can be taking place

- building on the child's existing language skills and other learning experiences

- building confidence by giving appropriate responsibility

- presenting learning activities as small steps likely to be understood and achieved

- remembering that praise acts as a motivating source for future success.

Discussions about the child's progress should take place regularly in these early stages with observations feeding into these discussions and then used to provide the basis for future planning. Successful strategies in communication and learning should be noted and then built on and extended with all the staff working in the same direction.

Philippe settled in happily in his setting for the first few days. He then became very anxious about coming to nursery and his parents found it very difficult to persuade him to come each morning. The bilingual nursery assistant talked with Philippe and his parents and discovered that it was the start of the day which was worrying him. He did not know what he would be doing or where his friends would be. It was decided that he would come to nursery, be greeted by his key person or be told the name of another member of staff who would meet him and then he would help them to set up the construction area and spend the first part of his morning playing there. After three weeks he no longer needed this support and made a happy start to his day at nursery.

Using the child's first language in school and at home

An important reason for supporting the child's first language is that from the child's viewpoint it is a familiar point of reference and one that offers a feeling of comfort and contact with previous events. In many ways the child is building two cultural identities, and both need to be supported. When an assessment of the child's language ability is made, it is important to assess both English and the language used at home if a full picture is to be formed of the child's language competence. The child may wish to use their first language when discussing family experiences and cultural events. If the setting does not have a bilingual member of staff, it may be possible to have some initial support from a member of the local community or from a parent who speaks the child's first language. In all positive nursery experiences plans are made to meet the individual needs of young children and the emerging bilingual child has particular needs at this time. Using the child's first language knowledge such as in a story will enable them to enjoy and understand the same story in English especially when accompanied by illustrations. Dual-language books are also a useful way of presenting stories. Bilingual children know that staff and other children have enjoyed the story even if all the words are not completely understood. They can enjoy the discussion and other activities which may follow, and listen and join in especially if there are related activities such as action songs or puppet activities.

Ways of supporting the child's first language and cultural identity include:

- seeing and understanding welcoming signs and key events in the first language

- finding their own name, written in first language script if appropriate, among the group names

- enjoying taped stories in the first language accompanied by the relevant picture book

- with other children, using culturally relevant resources such as musical instruments

- encouraging references to previous experiences and learning, and responding positively to these.

The child will naturally want to use their preferred language at home. It is a good sign of the child feeling well settled if there is communication by the child to parents about the activities that have taken place in school. A later stage of English language acquisition will come when the child is heard using both languages and uses the vocabulary that most easily comes to mind. This indicates an interaction and transfer between the languages, which will also occur later with ideas, knowledge and concepts. There are several organisations that have websites containing material to support language development including the teaching and learning of English as an additional language and bilingualism. Some of these include:

www.cilt.org.uk – National Centre for Languages

www.naldic.org.uk – National Association for Language Development

www.bfinclusion.org.uk – Bracknell Forest Inclusion website.

An overview of the Early Years Foundation Stage curriculum

In England and Northern Ireland staff plan learning activities based on the Early Years Foundation Stage curriculum. In Scotland planning is based on the appropriate parts of the Curriculum for Excellence and in Wales the Foundation Phase. In each curriculum the areas for learning are similar but not organised in exactly the same way. In England the framework for the early years curriculum uses the following headings:

- Personal, social and emotional development

- Communication, language and literacy

- Problem solving, reasoning and numeracy

- Knowledge and understanding of the world

- Physical development

- Creative development.

The Early Years Foundation Stage will be mandatory in September 2008, and offers provision for children from birth to 5 years of age with the purpose of building on the framework's four overarching themes – the unique child, positive relationships, the environment, and learning and development. Planning for learning is for all children including the emerging bilingual children. These children will be naturally acquiring their additional language through play and other planned and spontaneous activities some of which will be child-led and others adult-led. The *Practice Guidance to the Early Years Foundation Stage Framework* makes specific reference to provision for children with English as an additional language: 'Encourage parents whose children are learning English as an additional language to continue to encourage use of the first language at home (DfES, 2007: 42)' (QCA/DfES, 2000: 19).

Staff supporting the emerging bilingual child will use all aspects of the curriculum to develop language and be sensitive to opportunities to introduce, repeat and consolidate vocabulary, phrases and language structures. In this way the child is learning language within a purposeful and meaningful context.

Summary: key principles for laying good foundations for language learning

- It is essential to provide a welcoming and reassuring environment for young children and their families.

- Valuing children's first language and culture will enable them to make progress in English.

- First language skills should be actively promoted and these skills will transfer to additional languages.

- Promoting children's holistic development enables staff to support additional language skills.

- Parents and staff working together provide consistency and security for children.

- The role of the key worker is to assist children in making effective transitions.

- All children are entitled to benefit from the Early Years Foundation Stage curriculum.

CHAPTER

2 Capturing the interest of children

This chapter discusses the importance of play and building on the children's own interests in the language development of young children learning English as an additional language.

- Early childhood experiences
- Tuning in to children
- Children as good communicators
- Creating a nurturing learning environment
- Ways in which children learn best
- The young child as an active learner
- Using a theme-based approach to meet the language learning needs of children.

Early childhood experiences

Children have different experiences in their early childhood – some will have many happy childhood experiences playing and experimenting, while others may have a more limited range of experiences. These children will need to be able to enjoy a wide range of first-hand experiences in which first and additional language activities can be embedded.

During daily nursery activities children who are new to the setting will be learning from their peers in a reassuring environment. They will hear everyday English phrases modelled for them by children with whom they are playing. Young children do not need to learn English through meaningless vocabulary lists but, rather, in short chunks of language that are relevant to them. Because of the context, they can make sense of what they are hearing and try it out when ready. They feel part of the group and are not being isolated or made to feel different. Skilled practitioners need to observe the children's play and to note the children's interests and their readiness to communicate in English. At this point the children need plenty of support and opportunities to repeat and practise new phrases. If the imaginative play area is organised as a shop the children will hear greetings and phrases such as 'Good Morning', 'Hello' and 'What do you want?', 'What would you like?', 'Goodbye'. These everyday phrases can be used on a daily basis when welcoming and working with the children in the classroom. Repetition in a relevant context offers children chances to consolidate their learning and feel proud of their achievements. The imaginative play area also provides the opportunity to include culturally relevant resources that can be helpful to children learning about their new culture, and on other occasions to offer all children the motivation to learn about cultures different from their own.

Tuning in to young children

Tuning in to the needs of young children allows relationships to be built and strengthened. Staff working with young children need to hone their observational skills to understand and assess the particular needs of individual children. They then need to respond appropriately to these needs. On some occasions this will be to extend learning and then, at other times, to recognise that children can quickly become tired and need more restful activities. Working and playing in a new environment can be immensely tiring for children and, adding to these factors others such as striving to communicate in a new language and puzzling out different ways of participating and behaving, it is unsurprising that children require less demanding activities. It is as if the children have to switch off, and at these times staff will need to offer activities that can be achieved at a slower pace. It is better to offer activities that are still linked to those undertaken by the rest of the children in the group. Through quiet, independent activities, supported if necessary by a sensitive adult, the child will still feel involved and included but able to recharge their batteries. Drawing, sequencing pictures and listening to a first-language story tape are all worthwhile activities that can be carried out at the individual's own pace. Small-world play is good to maintain links with the main activity but one where the child's first language could accompany their play particularly if another child or group of children shared the same language. On some occasions staff may find it difficult to understand what a child is trying to communicate. Children learning their first language experience frustration when adults are unable to tune in to their needs and this is intensified for young bilingual learners.

Charlotte, aged two years, enjoyed listening to *Where does Thursday go?* by Janeen Brian and delighted in the illustrations by Stephen Michael King. She felt particularly inspired by the evocative pictures, learning about and enjoying the adventures of Splodge and his friend, Humbug. Shortly after first being introduced to this book she kept saying 'oogle gurgle, oogle gurgle', which was the sound of the river gurgling under the bridge. This was her way of asking for another reading of the book but unfortunately it took some time for her parents to tune in and make this link and she experienced some frustrating times. *Where does Thursday go?* is well worth a place in the class library and will be enjoyed by all children. For children learning English as an additional language there is repetition, rhyme, pictures full of interest as a basis for discussion and, on a more mundane level, an introduction to the days of the week. Splodge celebrates his birthday with balloons, birthday cake and candles, and enjoys many exciting adventures all of which provide starting points for many learning activities.

Children make enormous strides in their language and enjoy communicating and practising their new language skills, and the use of their first language at this stage is essential for all children.

Children as good communicators

It is quite likely that children starting at nursery will be good communicators in their first language. It is important for staff to assess their first language development and to build on these existing skills. The fact that the children may initially remain silent and not appear to participate should not be taken as an absence of language. This is a very normal situation and is often referred to as a 'silent period'.

Communication takes place in many ways not just through spoken language. Babies make their views felt and wishes known long before their first word. Observant staff should be alert for the first signs of participation from young bilingual children. This could be a small smile at a shared activity in circle time, a completed picture offered to a member of staff for praise and comment or a hand grasped and taken to the story corner. Body language and facial gesture can inform staff of children's anxiety or puzzlement and the need to have these issues addressed. In a busy nursery frequent and detailed observation can be difficult but is so important for the well-being of the children. When these first signs of understanding have been observed, the children can be invited to join in with easy responses that may have been previously modelled by other children or staff. As always, encouragement and support in these early stages is vital.

Young bilingual children may well have had a rich variety of language experiences at home or in another setting through joining in songs, games, action rhymes and stories. Equally other children may not have had this good a foundation and will need to be offered these experiences. As with all children and their language development, each child should have their individual needs met and a rich variety of first-hand experiences is the bedrock on which progress will be built. Evidence suggests that the way in which the emerging bilingual child moves forward with English is very similar to the way in which children make progress with their first language. However, when children have enjoyed oral language activities in their first language and their prior learning is recognised and built on, then progress in their new language may be quicker. Motivation and feeling comfortable in the new learning environment are key factors in progress.

When possible young bilingual children will benefit from group activities where there is another child who shares their first language. Parents need to be reassured that this will not hinder their learning of English but will in fact speed the process. An appropriate role for parents is to continue to assist their child in acquiring their first language and to discuss activities and ideas in this language, which will then help the concepts being developed in nursery. Children benefit when there is close communication between home and school and when themes and projects can be shared. Dual-language texts are particularly beneficial in this instance as parents and bilingual staff can introduce the story, discuss the characters and the events, look at the illustrations and carry out appropriate follow-up activities such as small-world play or creative play. When the same book is shared with the entire group, the bilingual children will have heard and understood the story and will be able to make links with the phrases and language used in the English version. Stories which use repetition are particularly useful. Good illustrative material helps the children to make these links as well as adding to the enjoyment of the story.

Jill and the Beanstalk is a traditional tale adapted by Manju Gregory and illustrated by David Anstey. This dual-language text is translated into Polish by Sophia Bac. The children may be familiar with the traditional version of the story – *Jack and the Beanstalk* – and will enjoy the rhyme and the rhythm of this adaptation. The story is ideal for a simple dramatic interpretation with the repetition of the giant's command 'Goose, deliver', and role-play opportunities in Jill, Jill's mum and Jill's brother Jack. Within this story there are references to well-known nursery rhymes such as 'Jack and Jill', 'Little Bo Peep' and 'Hickory Dickory Dock'. These give opportunities for extension activities as do the linked story props, Big Book, e-book, board games and puppets. Information about these resources can be found at www.mantralingua.com who also publishes the book. They also have an excellent book *Tom and Sofia start school* by Henriette Barkins in English and several languages including Polish, Chinese and Urdu.

Communication is not just through the spoken word and early years staff have many opportunities to offer other ways of encouraging communication. Drawing, painting and model-making are everyday nursery activities which give bilingual children the power of expressing their thoughts and feelings. Dance and movement not only offer these opportunities but also the enjoyment of working with other children where language is not such an important issue. Music-making is great fun and can encompass feelings of happiness and frustration. Where children can be seen to have a real interest in these expressive activities, staff can provide a way into the development of English through discussion and linked stories and rhymes.

Creating a nurturing learning environment

The attitude and approach of staff to young children are key factors in offering a nurturing environment in which to learn. This is important for all children, especially those who are new to their setting. Staff need to be aware of the importance of scaffolding language. This is when the context clues the child into the meaning and staff gradually add to the child's language efforts to extend their ability and understanding.

For example, when getting ready to play outside the children are encouraged to put on their outdoor clothes. 'Remember to put on your red, woolly hat as it's cold outside.' The child reaches for his hat and begins to link red and woolly with his hat. Red is assimilated into his vocabulary and may appear when next carrying out some painting activity.

Emerging bilingual children are motivated to learn English initially for social purposes and then to enable them to benefit from the everyday curriculum activities. Staff need to plan a learning environment where the children's first language is valued, encouraged and maintained while positively developing English. Although this is not an easy task it can be achieved by developing English language skills in similar ways to the ones used by parents in encouraging their children's language. First-hand experiences become the focus for talk and then these are built on and extended, moving from the concrete to the abstract.

To enable the children to feel happily settled and ready to learn, there are some practical issues that can support the children. If the children are able to use some English phrases to manoeuvre their way through the nursery day, they at once feel part of the nursery and can also experience a justified sense of pride in their achievements. Being able to count to 10 is a useful activity and can be learnt in a very natural way through songs and stories.

There are many number songs including:

1, 2, 3, 4, 5–once I caught a fish alive,
6, 7, 8, 9, 10–then I let him go again.
Why did you let him go?
Because he bit my finger so
Which finger did he bite?
This little finger on the right.

This song can be accompanied by suitable actions and the first enthusiastic participation in English for some children will be the miming of the biting action of the fish.

A dual-language text which would support the learning of numbers 1 to 10 is *Handa's Hen*. This story by Eileen Browne, translated into Hindi by Awadesh Misra, gives a wonderful insight into the animal life of Kenya with the Citrus Swallowtail Butterfly and Striped Grass Mouse. Moreover, it is an interesting way of reinforcing counting as Handa and her friend Akayo go in search of her Grandma's black hen. Along the way they encounter 'two fluttery butterflies', 'three stripy mice' and many other animals until they come across 10 chicks and of course one black hen!

It would be helpful for staff to learn to count to 10 in the bilingual child's first language so that the child will be understood when using either language. Staff should take care to be able to pronounce and write the child's name correctly and help all the children in the class to be able to do the same.

The use of the visual timetable can provide support for all children, not only those learning English as an additional language. The website hosted by the *Times Educational Supplement* has some excellent picture cards in its resource bank, which can be downloaded for use in creating a visual timetable – www.tes.co.uk. Choose simple, clear symbols for the daily key points of the nursery day. Discuss with the children the reason for the choice of symbols – some children will be able to suggest symbols that are meaningful to them. Laminate the clearly drawn symbols and attach some Velcro to the back of the card. Have another piece of cardboard ready complete with a horizontal Velcro strip. Discuss with the children the order of events for the morning and then, at an appropriate time the afternoon, activities, and ask the children to arrange the symbols accordingly. Refer frequently to the symbols using the correct vocabulary. The children will soon make links with the symbol and the activity and, more importantly, they will be able to find reassurance in the predictability of their day. Use can also be made of colour and shape in choosing the card for the symbols.

Staff can use various strategies to provide a nurturing environment. Sensitive grouping of children can ensure that there is a supportive friend or buddy who will model language for the bilingual children to copy. Their friend can also guide them through the various social and cultural situations that they may find puzzling. Staff can ensure that bilingual children are placed in a position so that they can hear clearly, can observe any accompanying gestures and can always see any book illustrations or visual material that is supporting the language used. The use of photographs, models, pictures and video material can be helpful to all children. In turn-taking games, place the bilingual child third or fourth in the group so that they can copy what is required. Have high expectations for all children but also appreciate that any 'non-compliance' on the part of the bilingual child is perhaps a matter of not understanding rather than a withdrawal of cooperation.

All children have an entitlement to benefit from the Early Years Foundation Stage, and context is a key factor in helping bilingual children learn sufficient English to enable them to do so. Scaffolding language provides a supportive structure for them. First-hand experiences provide the context and the motivation for children to learn language in a way that is meaningful to them. They gain in confidence and make their first tentative steps in English. Their first words are added to by staff who provide a rich commentary on the children's play and learning activities. The children gain an understanding of their new language and practise and recognise words and hear the patterns of intonation and emphasis; in short, they are tuning in to English and in time will rely less on concrete experiences for their language progress.

Ways in which children learn best

The *Practice Guidance for the Early Years Foundation Stage* clearly sets out the principles that underpin good early years practice (DfES, 2007: 6–7). These principles are closely allied to the ways in which young children will learn English as an additional language in the most effective and enjoyable manner. Early years practitioners need to be able to implement these principles in their own setting and to be clear about why they do what they do. Pressure can be applied, by people who do not truly understand how young children develop, to teach them English 'by rote' to achieve seemingly quick results but this argument needs to be rejected with clear explanations. Teaching English as an additional language is not just about achieving successful language outcomes; it is also about exploring a new culture, having positive attitudes about learning, feeling good about their identity in their new environment and making progress in all aspects of the early years curriculum.

Children learn English as an additional language best when:

- they are given support in their first language so that these skills transfer to English language acquisition

- they are positively encouraged to make contributions in their first language

- first-hand experiences are planned to offer a rich foundation for talk

- opportunities are given for practice and repetition of newly learnt phrases

- play is valued as central to children's language development

- their efforts are valued as well as their achievements

- they are given sufficient time to make a response which may not be an oral one

- they are given appropriate responsibility which initially does not require too much language input

- they are part of a group which provides support, motivation and challenge

- early years staff are aware that they must clearly model the language to be learnt.

Staff can support these principles by planning to sensitively include emerging bilingual children from their very first day in the classroom. The children need to feel included with the general activities of the nursery and not singled out by withdrawing them from the setting or by having completely different tasks to complete. Tasks need to be clearly explained and demonstrated, purposeful and build on the children's existing knowledge and skills. Learning is best achieved when it is in small 'chunks' that can be achieved followed by encouragement and praise. Resources that are culturally relevant to the first language can provide reassurance, motivation and interest. The local community or local authority support staff can help with the loan of relevant resources. It is important to share the plans and ideas with all staff with whom the children will come in contact so that, when appropriate, an all-round evaluation of progress can be made.

The young child as an active learner

Young children learn through being active in both a physical and intellectual sense. They need to be involved and responsible for their learning so that all their energy and enthusiasm is harnessed and channelled into the activity. There is tremendous job satisfaction and reward in teaching young children, partly due to their energetic approach and sense of wonder as they pursue their current interests. Good early years practice ensures that there are plenty of practical experiences that they can engage with alongside and with other children and adults. Cooking is an excellent activity which can promote all aspects of development within the Early Years Foundation Stage. Staff must remember to observe all the setting's policies with regard to health, hygiene, safety and any child's allergic reactions to certain foods. Help the children to get into the right habits from the start and explain to them the reasons for correct hand-washing, clearing up and being prepared to try and taste new foods! Exploit every opportunity to talk about what is happening, to introduce new vocabulary and phrases and encourage the children to comment and contribute in their first and additional languages.

Promoting all aspects of development through a cooking activity with young children

■ Personal, social and emotional development – working with another child to cook a delicious and tasty offering which is then shared with others in the nursery and at home. Children experience a sense of pride and achievement and find out about the ingredients and recipes of other countries. Health and safety issues are discussed, and children learn about working in a safe and hygienic manner.

■ Communication, language and literacy – a wealth of new expressions are learnt. Children can comment on what they are doing and hear words that are specific to actions such as mixing, spooning and pouring. Their range of vocabulary is increased as new words are used appropriately in a context that enables the children to understand their meaning. Recipes are followed, and understanding these can be simplified through the use of symbols and pictures.

■ Problem solving, reasoning and numeracy – opportunities to weigh and measure volume, to estimate and judge capacity and to hear and use mathematical language such as more than and less than. A simple bar chart can be made to record the children's preferences after they have tasted the food.

■ Knowledge and understanding of the world – there are many scientific ideas to find out about in cooking activities such as bread-making. Children learn to work with a range of cookery equipment and ingredients from different parts of the world. They observe changes in the ingredients as they are mixed together and perhaps cooked.

■ Physical development – children have the opportunity to improve hand–eye co-ordination and control as they pour liquid from one container to another or transfer ingredients from a larger container to a smaller one. If healthy recipes are used, children are learning about nutritious foods and the part they play in growth and development.

■ Creative development – cooking is a creative activity which, although based on a particular recipe, gives plenty of scope for choice and originality such as choosing the pizza topping or the shape of the cutter for the biscuits. Remember that the children will have their own preferences and the outcome may not look exactly as the adult intended! Talk with the children about their decisions and choices and what they like or do not like. Photograph or draw the tasty result and use it to create a class book about cooking.

It is better to work with very small groups of children in an organised and unhurried atmosphere. The children need to be as active and as involved as possible. The use of knives must be supervised closely or, in some instances, the task carried out by the adult. Always teach or demonstrate the safe use of knives using the claw method (one hand cutting with the other hand holding the ingredient and all fingers out of the way) or the bridge method (one hand cutting 'under the bridge' with the other hand holding the ingredient in a bridge shape). Other than this the children should have the responsibility of carrying out all activity.

Making fruit kebabs is a good start to a cookery project. Use as many different fruits as possible and talk about their country of origin, the colour and shape of the fruit and do not forget to discuss what it tastes like! Help the children to look for the sequence patterns that are repeated in the fruits or colours as they are placed on the kebab skewer.

Tasty fruit kebabs

What is needed:	Wooden kebab skewers, knives, chopping boards, greaseproof paper and aprons.
	Fruit.
What to do:	Discuss with the children the names of the fruit and their colour.
	Cut the fruit into small chunks.
	Encourage the children to choose which fruits they will use.
	Each child puts a selection of fruit on to the skewer repeating the name of the fruit as it is placed.
	Each child arranges their kebabs on a plate.

To obtain maximum learning and language value from this activity it would be ideal to take some of the children to the supermarket to shop for the ingredients. The journey to the supermarket will provide plenty of opportunity to discuss the proposed activity in English and in the children's first language, and for the adult to support the children's actions with appropriate language. Remember that any visit of this sort is an opportunity for the children to say 'Hello', 'Please' and 'Thank you'. They may need to be reminded, practise and then be given time to participate. Help the children to choose the fruit, pay for it and carry it back. Talk about the activity with all the children and encourage the children who visited the supermarket to give an account of their visit, with appropriate staff support.

The shopping activity could be extended through using the imaginative play area and equipping it as a supermarket or greengrocer's shop with 'fruit'. Be ready to support the children with the names of the fruit and saying 'Please' and 'Thank you', using the proper greetings and encouraging them to speak clearly and confidently.

Using a theme-based approach to meet the language learning needs of children

Young children's learning is not compartmentalised. Learning thrives in an environment where there is a balance between adult-led and child-initiated activities. On some occasions there will be a need for direct teaching and at other times skilful building on children's interests to acquire new knowledge and skills or to have the opportunity to practise existing skills and to transfer knowledge to different situations. Themes or projects which are meaningful and of great interest to children allow time for ideas and concepts to be established and then to develop in a variety of directions, some of which may not have been in the original planning document but nevertheless have real learning potential. On these occasions the enthusiasm and energy of the children inject breathtaking momentum into the project and staff can see the true potential of children's abilities and creativity. It is at times like these that working with young children gives personal and professional satisfaction!

All children are able to participate at different levels, and for emerging bilingual children they are able to gain different cultural perspectives and contribute experiences from their own culture. The children's first and additional language needs have to be identified and supported and topic work enables all the children in the class to learn some words in different languages. For some children topic work may be a new way of working and careful observation is needed to ensure that learning is taking place.

Project work is also an opportunity for parents and members of the local community to be welcomed to the classroom to share skills and experiences with all children. Parents may be willing to read dual-language books or demonstrate a skill such as origami. Activities which are visual, do not rely too much on language ability and can be carried out by the children perhaps at a less complicated level are good choices.

> Keiko was able to learn about shape, colour and number as she took part in the Ollie the Octopus game which was part of the planning for the sea theme. The early years practitioner drew a large octopus and numbered each tentacle. At the end of each tentacle he placed a square or circular shaped card in different colours. Keiko watched the children throw a dice and say 'Ollie the Octopus needs a yellow square on his number 2 tentacle' and place a correctly matching card from the spare pile on the correct tentacle. Initially she just put the correct card in the right place without saying anything. She soon learnt the vocabulary for the colours, shapes and numbers and was very proud that she could join in the game so easily. Her next step was to be able to say the whole phrase, with staff support, just like the other children.

Themes are excellent for providing a meaningful context for new vocabulary and phrases to be to introduced and practised. The theme provides the context for scaffolding enabling language learning to make good progress. Basic concepts such as number, colour and shape can be reintroduced in each topic and learning about them gains new momentum in a different context. Well-loved themes include:

- transport

- toys

- weather

- seasons

- sea.

Each theme can be considered from a multicultural perspective and the problem may well be not what to include but what to leave out. When carrying out the planning, in addition to thinking about curriculum requirements, remember to introduce key vocabulary that bilingual children can use in the daily classroom and home-based activities. Model sentences and phrases, and give time for the children to hear them several times and perhaps use them in the appropriate context. Sensitive grouping will encourage the emerging bilingual child to copy their peers and to feel a part of the class activity. Themes naturally have spin-offs into linked mini topics and offer staff and children space to share their own interest and expertise which develops self-esteem and self-confidence.

Within the framework of the theme there can be many opportunities to promote language-rich play. Strategies such as the use of story sacks, story aprons, small-world play, theme trays, class books, puppets and the imaginative play area can be adapted to link in with the chosen theme. Collecting relevant resources is a key factor in any successful and sustained topic. Parents, the local community, friends and relatives can be particularly helpful. It is worth spending some time collecting resources at the planning stage so that staff know what they have to work with and what, if any, vital ingredients still have to be found.

Summary: key principles to encourage children to be interested in their language learning

- First-hand experiences are central to children's language learning.

- Staff who are sensitive to children's needs can respond appropriately.

- Language is only one method of communication used by young children.

- Staff who create a nurturing learning environment enable children to acquire sound foundations for language progress.

- Children need to be actively involved in their learning.

- Themes and projects can build on children's interests as well as meeting curriculum requirements.

---

3 Getting started!

This chapter offers some strategies for settings where there are few children who are learning English as an additional language and ideas for developing practice in settings where there are many children and families from diverse language backgrounds.

■ Getting everybody on board
■ Teamwork
■ Creating an inclusive environment
■ Settling in to the new environment.

Getting everybody on board

Early years practitioners are becoming very used to working within a multi-professional framework. Children's centres offer children and parents a range of services. Nurseries are organised to provide integrated care and education, and childminders work with health and education specialists to provide the very best for young children. Nursery schools increasingly offer childcare services before and after traditional school hours. All settings are extending their range of services to families. They endeavour to meet the needs of all families in terms of languages and culture.

The National Professional Qualification in Integrated Centre Leadership (NPQICL) is the first national programme for leaders within multi-agency, early years settings. The qualification seeks to equip course participants with the skills and knowledge to work in partnership with professionals in the community who are delivering a range of services to young children and their families. For families who have children learning English as an additional language this should, in time, ensure that all of their health, educational and social needs are identified and met. Some settings will have many languages and cultures represented in their nursery and have diversity clearly embedded in all their practice, while other settings may just have one or two children and their families speaking languages other than English within the group and are beginning to think about how to embrace different languages and cultures.

Each setting will want to organise the support and teaching for children learning English as an additional language in different ways but each setting will find it helpful to appoint a member of staff who will be responsible for this aspect of curriculum development.

Different job titles used for the member of staff leading the programme include:

- bilingual co-ordinator

- intercultural leader

- English as an additional language specialist

- bilingual advisory teacher.

The member of staff leading the development of English language teaching will need to formulate a plan which identifies priorities and ensures that members of the team are working in the most effective manner.

Writing a policy or action plan is a platform for researching and agreeing the approach and implementing ways of working with children and families. It clarifies ideas and provides a framework within which to work. It should be regarded as a working document written, implemented, evaluated and revised regularly, and used as a focus for staff to reflect on their work. In this way practice is evaluated and areas for improvement identified. Policies take time to write, as thinking and practice have to evolve and all members of staff need to be included. The policy co-ordinator or English as an additional language leader needs to collect contributions and ensure that consultation takes place with staff, parents, management committee or governors. The views of children need to be listened to and included where possible. Policy headings could include:

Rationale – the policy should set out the rationale for why the teaching of English as an additional language takes place in the way it does and the way in which it is embedded into the early years curriculum.

Aims and objectives – these clearly state the outcomes to be achieved so that they can be regularly monitored and evaluated.

Good practice – guidelines as to how the policy will be implemented are useful so that staff and parents know how the intended outcomes will be achieved. Within this section there can be guidelines with regard to:

- induction – ways in which children will be helped to settle and ways in which information about the children will be gathered

- partnership with parents – including strategies for communicating with parents and the ways in which they can become involved with their children's learning

- outreach activities – ways of working with members of the local community and setting up home visits

- resources – audited to monitor stereotyping and cultural diversity

- planning – long-term, medium-term and short-term planning which ensures a balance between adult-initiated and child-led activities and provides for first language and English language activities

- record-keeping – methods for keeping a language record as well as progress in other aspects of the curriculum

- assessment – ways in which first language and English activities will be assessed and how this information will be used to inform future planning. The schedule for observations and ways in which child observations will inform assessment and be used for planning purposes

- evaluation – regular evaluation of teaching and learning takes place and the information gained fed back into planning.

The policy needs to guide practice and is a useful tool in helping staff to work in the same direction. The policy also needs to state who will have the responsibility for ensuring various actions are carried out – describing the job role rather than individual members of staff. A time frame for actions should also be included, although this may have to be amended from time to time. Where possible, build on the strengths of staff members especially where English as an additional language is a new curriculum development.

Ideally, a setting would be able to employ bilingual language assistants with language skills relevant to the children in the setting. Where this is not possible an assistant may be employed on a peripatetic basis and spend one session each week in each setting. Part time contributions are extremely valuable and should be organised so that maximum benefit can be derived. Another option is to contact the local education department to seek support from the bilingual language service. These services can offer practical support and can also loan resources such as books and equipment that reflect cultural and linguistic diversity. These resources can be part of the learning and teaching that benefits all children in the setting.

Teamwork

In integrated centres or in nurseries a range of staff can be employed on a full- or part-time basis. All the staff enrich the children's experience but the staff have to be managed and their roles clearly defined.

Any nursery team involved with introducing English as an additional language could comprise some of the following practitioners:

- nursery teacher

- qualified early years practitioner

- language support teacher

- unqualified nursery assistant

- bilingual language staff

- student

- parent

- members of the local community who have first language expertise and act as interpreters.

The larger the team the more need there is for good communication and the sharing of information between team members. Additional adults in the nursery, when properly deployed, enable obstacles to learning to be overcome and the diverse needs of the children met as part of an inclusive environment. Good communication helps with team-building and encourages individuals to contribute their ideas. Not all members of the team will be able to attend every meeting and there need to be strategies to keep people informed and involved. Writing meeting minutes is useful or a central message book regularly used encourages contribution and innovation. All team members need to be aware of the requirement for confidentiality as personal family information will often be shared as it forms an important part of the children's background.

The role of bilingual staff

Bilingual language staff are invaluable in enabling children learning English as an additional language to take part in all nursery activities as soon as possible. They are of great help to children, parents and other staff. A bilingual member of staff will be able to:

- accompany staff on home visits to meet the children and parents

- share information about the children's first language usage, culture and religious practice

- explain the routine activities of the nursery in the first language to provide reassurance and understanding for the children

- check children's understanding of the choices and activities offered to them

- listen to children so that their ideas, concerns and feelings can be expressed

- explain to other children about first languages, cultural and religious practice

- monitor the effectiveness of the induction programme co-ordinating child observations

- carry out child observations particularly those requiring first language input

- work with all groups of children from different language backgrounds

- provide opportunities to use and extend children's first language skills

- introduce greetings and some other simple first language vocabulary to the other children and encourage their use

- read and tell first-language and dual-language stories, rhymes and poems

- give advice on culturally appropriate and relevant tasks

- prepare the context for nursery activities using the child's first language

- participate appropriately in activities scaffolding language so that children gain in confidence

- support the development of concepts in the first language as these will transfer to additional languages

- contribute to the assessment of progress particularly in first-language skills

- provide support to children learning English as an additional language during whole-group times such as circle time, lunch time and playtime

- be a positive role model

- assist with effective communication between home and nursery through meetings, letters and phone calls.

At the beginning of the nursery school year there were many new children in the group including a high proportion of children learning English as an additional language. The teacher regularly discussed with the children the guidelines that would be drawn up to ensure that everybody was able to play and learn happily in the classroom and also outdoors. She told the children that the guidelines would be their 'Golden Rules'. She used words and examples that were understood by the children, and the bilingual member of staff added further explanation. All the children made contributions in English and/or in their first language. Reasons for the agreed behaviour were discussed and emphasis was given to thinking about how all children and adults were different and liked to do things in different ways. As the children agreed each aspect of the guidelines, it was written up in English and in the children's home language. All the children drew pictures which linked with relevant scenarios, and the bilingual staff worked with the children to enable them to express thoughts in their first language. These ideas were shared with all the children. Eventually a display was created using all the children's contributions and frequent reference was made so that the guidelines could be remembered. This display was shown to parents and any of their queries answered. Gradually all the children could understand the guidelines in English.

It is important to remember that, like any member of the team, bilingual staff may need guidance for them to carry out their role in a professional and effective manner. Depending on their qualifications and level of experience, the following support will be of help:

- Provide a full induction programme for staff which covers all the setting's policy documents allowing them time to meet other staff and the opportunity to discuss policies and how these will affect their job role.

- Enable bilingual staff to have time to build relationships with staff, children and parents, particularly those for whom they have direct responsibility.

- Ensure they are familiar with all routine nursery activities and what their role will normally be at these times.

- Be clear about the ways that they should work with parents and the strategies that are in place for regular two-way communication.

- Explain how child observations will be organised and how information from the observations will be recorded.

- Plan opportunities for staff to support children's first language skills and how assessment of these skills will take place and be shared with other staff.

- Build in regular opportunities to discuss their role and listen to ideas for improving the teaching and learning strategies related to English as an additional language.

- Plan curriculum activities with staff so that they have time to prepare their contribution and become familiar with the resources and equipment to be used by all the children.

- Encourage staff to become involved with all groups of children, not only children learning English as an additional language.

- Ensure they know that their role is appreciated and valued.

The role of an interpreter

The use of an interpreter from the local community may be necessary for settings where there are no bilingual staff or where there are just one or two children learning English as an additional language. An interpreter could be used during the first few weeks of the children's induction and be invaluable for helping the children to settle and reduce parents' concerns. They must work closely to the guidelines provided by nursery staff. Some interpreters may be used to working with children in early years settings, while others could be inexperienced and initially daunted by the busy, seemingly chaotic but purposeful environment. The main role of the interpreter is to help the children adjust to their new environment and to provide feedback to the nursery staff. Their tasks could be very wide ranging, including:

■ meeting and greeting children, parents and carers at the beginning of the day to find out if there is any important information that needs to be passed to nursery staff

■ explaining the curriculum activities and choices open to the children

■ supporting the children through routine daily events and answering their questions

■ communicating the ideas and feelings of children to their peers and to nursery staff enabling children to fully participate in the nursery day

■ providing information to parents and carers about the activities of the day and giving any necessary information about activities that are planned for the children's next visit.

It is important for the children learning English as an additional language not to become dependent on the person acting as an interpreter, and this needs careful explanation and management by nursery staff. The interpreter may not be familiar with early years care and education and may translate literally, in which case some real meaning may be lost. When working with an interpreter and meeting parents, nursery staff need to remember that the meeting is with the parents and that the discussion is with them and not the interpreter. Keep the discussion to the main important points and deliver these in short chunks that the interpreter can remember and translate. Allow plenty of time for parents to participate in the discussion and keep in mind the fact that for some parents the whole ethos of the nursery and the place of play in children's learning may be new to them. Where possible have some visual materials such as nursery equipment, photographs, short video film snippets and relevant examples of the children's work to explain the points being discussed. At the end of the meeting recap the main points briefly and ask the interpreter to check that there are no other aspects which the parents wish to mention and that they have fully understood what has been discussed.

Creating an inclusive environment

In order to create a truly inclusive and welcoming environment for children and their families it is important for all staff to understand the principles of equality of opportunity and to actively promote these principles in their practice. Staff who work with young children need to have responsibility for their own practice but they also have responsibility for developing positive attitudes regarding gender, disability, ethnicity and cultural differences. Young children begin to develop their concepts of beliefs, identity and culture as young as 3 years of age. Their first-hand experiences will depend in part on the diversity in the local community but the early years curriculum can offer many opportunities to broaden children's experiences of language and culture. A multilingual and multicultural environment affirms bilingual children's experiences and learning and offers new experiences to children who are monolingual. A theme such as 'Myself' is a good starting point to share experiences, celebrations and family life with peers, and to understand that there are many similarities but also some differences in the way families do things. It is much better for a wide range of cultural experiences to be part of the day-to-day curriculum rather than 'add on' activities. Circle time is an appropriate occasion to explore the children's ideas and to answer openly their questions about race, ethnicity and religion at an appropriate level for their understanding. This level can best be gauged by listening carefully to their questions and answering them honestly.

A group of 4-year-old children were sitting with a member of staff discussing how they could make sure all of them had someone to play with and that no one was left without any friends. They talked about how it felt to think that they might be left on their own and why they felt unhappy at these times. They mentioned reasons why they might not want to play with some children because they were different and liked doing things in their own way and could not always understand what was being said. The children discussed how to share toys, play together, think about each other's feelings and take turns in games. The member of staff reminded the children about the similarities between the children and all the things that they enjoyed doing together. The session ended with a reading of *Best friends, Special friends*, written and illustrated by Susan Rollings, with the children enjoying the rhyming text and agreeing that friends look and behave very differently from each other.

Each setting should have an equality of opportunity policy and code of practice that are regularly reviewed and updated, with opportunities for staff to take part in professional development opportunities. The review process is important to record any relevant issues that have taken place in the previous year and to enable staff and children to discuss misunderstandings and disagreements. For children these discussions should take place when needed rather than left to a particular time in the review process.

Equality of opportunity and inclusion are at the heart of good early years practice and make a statement of commitment to all children and their families that they will have full access to the education, care and services that are offered in the setting. In an inclusive environment first-language skills and diversity are celebrated and racism, prejudice and stereotyping are properly challenged. Achievements by all children outside the nursery should be recognised and valued and shared with peers during relevant curriculum activities. The *Practice Guidance for the Early Years Foundation Stage* provides a clear statement as to the importance of anti-discriminatory practice: 'You must promote positive attitudes to diversity and difference within all children. Practitioners must plan for the needs of children from black and other minority ethnic backgrounds, including those learning English as an additional language, and for the needs of any children with learning difficulties or disabilities' (DfES, 2007: 6). Evidence shows that in settings where staff and children are able to appreciate and value diversity then children learning English as an additional language are more likely to integrate into the nursery and take part more readily in the curriculum activities.

When children learning English as an additional language initially come to the nursery with their parents, the first impressions they have of the setting as an inclusive environment are crucial. This can be a very anxious time for parents as well as the children, depending on their own educational experiences and their familiarity with early years care and education in this country. Some education authorities have videos that can be borrowed to show some of the key features of early years care and education in England. There are several ways of demonstrating a welcoming and inclusive environment including:

- making sure that the member of staff making the home visit is accompanied if necessary by a bilingual member of the nursery

- offering all parents information about the nursery in formats that are helpful to them so that they can prepare their children for their nursery education

- informing parents of the various communication strategies that have been organised for them so that they know about their children's progress and can discuss any concerns or aspects of their child's education that are particularly enjoyable or beneficial

- inviting parents to a social event such as a coffee morning followed by a short tour of the setting. If possible make sure there is a crèche for younger children and babies and that parents are able to talk to people who share their home language

- communicating the relevant information about language, culture and previous educational experiences to all members of the nursery

- ensuring that visitor directions are easy to follow through the use of appropriate symbols or use of languages understood by all members of the nursery community

- planning activities so that the children can be included in the full range of nursery activities from the very first day

- ensuring that a member of staff who speaks the first language greets the children and family with a reassuring smile and an explanation of the daily nursery routine

- showing interest in the home language, giving it status in the nursery

- ensuring that labelling on display boards and the information on the parents' noticeboards includes all languages represented in the nursery

- displaying culturally relevant materials in a positive manner and using them appropriately in curriculum activities

- equipping the book areas with dual-language texts

- supporting parents who wish to have opportunities to read dual-language books to all children

- ensuring that the nursery reflects cultural and linguistic diversity in all aspects of learning such as examples of different scripts in the emergent writing area.

When staff in the nursery make every effort for the setting to be part of the local community, it is very likely that the expertise to be found in the community will be willingly shared with the children. Parents are less likely to feel isolated when they feel at ease and can join in with activities with other families sharing their first language. The nursery may be one of a range of settings within the community all of which can be a source of support and resources. Children may have previously attended a 'stay and play' group, visited the toy library or other 'drop in' group or they may have been cared for by a registered childminder. Older siblings may attend an after-school or breakfast club and any out of school holiday club. Parents might be able to attend the local further education college for English language classes or other socially based activities. All these community-based groups providing an inclusive environment enable members of the family to integrate into their new culture, become familiar with its customs and provide motivation to learn and improve English language skills.

Settling in to the new environment

Despite good planning and thorough preparation some children find it hard to adapt to their new setting. The speed at which children settle depends on their level of anxiety and previous experience in parting from their parent or carer, their previous 'away from home' experiences and their ability to communicate their needs. Nurseries will have different policies as to how long and in what ways parents are able to spend time in the nursery helping to settle their child. However, as soon as the parent is no longer in the nursery it becomes a matter of priority for the child to be able to communicate with staff. Where the child's first language is spoken by a member of staff this is easier but learning some English as soon as possible is useful. Some key vocabulary includes:

- greetings – 'Hello', 'Good morning', 'Good afternoon', 'Goodbye'.

- numbers – initially 1 to 10

- simple nursery activities – lunch time, circle time, mat time, group time, playtime

- colours – yellow, red, blue, green, white and black

- 'Please' and 'Thank you'

- 'Can I have … ?'

- 'I like … I don't like … '

- 'Where's the … ?'

- 'What's that … ?'

- 'I don't understand'

- 'What's this in English?'

Much of this useful vocabulary can be included and taught through songs. A nursery welcome and good bye song sung every day will soon be picked up by all the children. Nursery staff can model the vocabulary and phrases and use as many visual cues as possible.

A useful welcoming song to be sung to the tune of 'Merrily we roll along' is:

Good morning (Toby), good morning (Toby), good morning (Toby)
We welcome you today.

or

(Yuka) is at school today, school today, school today
(Yuka) is at school today
Please stay and play.

or as a goodbye song:

Goodbye (Sophia), goodbye (Sophia), goodbye (Sophia)
We'll see you again quite soon.

The home visit is an important part of helping children to enjoy their first days at nursery. Arrangements can be made during the home visit for the new children to begin at the nursery on different days so that the staff can spend sufficient time help-ing each child to settle in well. For schools this will normally be at the beginning of a term, in a day nursery or at a childminder this could be at any time of the year. Whatever the occasion, good preparation of the staff is paramount. Simple factors such as being able to pronounce the child's name correctly and greeting them in their first language can be important aspects in helping the child to enjoy coming to nursery.

Another priority for staff especially for key workers is to build trusting relationships. This includes relationships with the staff and the children, so that they feel secure and reassured as quickly as possible, and with their parents. The ways in which the nursery builds relationships with parents in the earliest days of their children's education affects the happiness and educational progress of their child and may also affect how the par-ents view the whole educational process through to secondary education and beyond. Staff are also instrumental in helping new children to build relationships with their peers. It is usually preferable for new children learning English to be placed in groups of children of the same age as this helps with the building of friendship groups. Children are more likely to learn everyday English from each other than from adults. They hear these everyday phrases repeated in a context which helps them to understand, and they enjoy being part of the group and joining in with activities and not feeling different from the other children.

Face-to-face meetings between staff and parents are essential for building warm relationships but it is also beneficial for there to be a written booklet containing vital information which is written in the parents' first language. The booklet provides a focus for the initial discussion and can help to alleviate some of the parents' feelings of isolation and worries about not knowing about the way the nursery 'works'. Some parents may feel intimidated and unable to attend any school events, contributing to further isolation. Having the information in writing in their first language enables the parent to refer to it when necessary and encourages discussion and further preparation with their child.

Useful detail includes:

Information for when the child starts

- times and dates when the nursery is open and closed

- names and roles of the staff at the nursery

- photographs of all staff

- the name of the child's key worker or class teacher

- arrangements for first language support such as the name of the bilingual support assistant

- arrangements for the first day including lunch arrangements

- a brief outline of regular daily activities

- the ways in which the children usually begin and end their day.

Ongoing information

- the ways in which children learn through play

- play and learning activities to be found in the nursery such as sand play and construction play

- the ways in which the child's first language can support the learning of English

- how parents can support their child's first-language development

- arrangements for borrowing books including dual-language texts

- ways in which parents can support children's learning such as visiting the library, enjoying songs and rhymes together and talking about the places visited together

- ways in which parents can become involved with their child's nursery education

- communication strategies in the parent's first language to exchange information between home and nursery

- arrangements for keeping parents informed about their child's progress

- details of any groups that meet regularly that could be of support to parents.

These initial discussions should include a two-way exchange of information so that the nursery has all relevant medical, cultural and religious information.

A booklet for the child composed mainly of photographs of the setting's activities is also a helpful introduction. The pictures of children in the setting playing, singing and enjoying stories are of interest and may enable a new child to ask questions about what their day in nursery will be like. Information about who their special 'buddies' will be and what activities they like provide a context for the child's questions. It is also helpful to provide a visual overview of the daily routine activities, perhaps using the symbols from the setting's visual timetable.

During the home visit one nursery ensures that the key worker and the bilingual nursery assistant take with them the booklet for the parent, the booklet for the child and a copy of *Spot goes to School* by Eric Hill in the relevant dual-language version.

This 'lift the flap' book is available in a wide range of dual-language texts.

Much loved Spot is welcomed to school by Miss Bear. There is much repetition of 'Hello' by the cheery hippo, tortoise, monkey and alligator who are Spot's school friends. The reader is gently led through familiar events in the school day including 'show and tell time', playtime, story time and, finally, home time, which happens much too early for Spot! As with all the Spot series, the illustrations are clearly drawn and of great appeal to young children who enjoy participating through the 'lift the flap' format.

This book is left with the family and is instrumental in helping parents discuss the activities and enjoyment connected with starting at nursery. When the children are in the nursery they see other Spot books and are reassured in seeing this link with home.

Summary: key principles for introducing English into an early years setting

- Involving all members of the team in additional language activities is essential.

- Written policies clarify ideas and help staff to adopt a consistent approach to their work.

- Employing bilingual staff enriches the experiences of all of the children.

- Equality of opportunity and inclusion are at the heart of good nursery practice.

- Building trusting relationships enables children to settle into their new environment.

CHAPTER 4

Planning for success

This chapter looks at how planning, observation and assessment can enable practitioners to focus on both planned and impromptu opportunities to promote language development for children learning English as an additional language. There is also a checklist for staff to review their practice and ensure how well emerging bilingual children are settling into their nursery.

- Getting to know children through observation
- Assessment as a celebration of children's achievements
- Planning the curriculum.

Getting to know children through observation

Observation needs to take place in circumstances where children feel as relaxed as possible with the observation part of naturally occurring activity during the nursery day. Over a period of time the observations should cover the six areas of the Foundation Stage curriculum, both adult-led and child-initiated activities and children taking part in activities indoors and outside. If children are recent arrivals in England as well as in the nursery, they will have particular needs that may not be apparent in children who have grown up in England but whose first language is not English. The first priority of staff is to begin to observe language development when children are settled in the nursery from an emotional and social viewpoint. When they are settled, the children will feel happy to communicate in many different ways. When they are not, these needs must be addressed before beginning to assess language skills. Use of the children's first language will contribute greatly to the children's social and emotional well-being.

Observation and assessment are part of the planning cycle in all early years settings. Child observation is a key tool in assessing children's all-round development and on some occasions in focusing on language development. The information gained from observation can be instrumental in helping newly arrived bilingual children become familiar with their setting. Effective observation enables the practitioner to find out about the children's interests, their achievements, their learning needs and learning styles. Staff begin to know the children well and understand the best ways in which to organise the learning environment.

The *Practice Guidance for the Early Years Foundation Stage* identifies observation as one of the principles for early years education: 'Observations help practitioners to decide where children are in their learning and development and to plan what to do. This is an essential part of daily practice in any setting, regardless of the age of the baby or child' (DfES, 2000: 11).

Observation needs to take place on an agreed regular basis and has to be part of the work schedule of staff. When a child first comes to nursery, short, weekly observations are helpful; the frequency can then be decreased to a full observation once every half-term unless a particular concern arises. If observation is not planned for and properly managed, then the other busy activities of nursery life tend to take preference and observation does not happen. These planned observations can be backed up by the more spontaneous observations that are taken because there is something important that has been noticed, such as a particular achievement, a critical event or an important verbal interaction between two of the children or with staff. These impromptu observations can perhaps be written in a small notebook, a sticky label or a large Post-it note which is then placed in the child's file. Well-planned observations carried out by trained staff can provide reliable assessment information on more than one aspect of the early years curriculum. A comprehensive understanding of child development, together with effective observation skills, should enable observations to be taken efficiently. The key worker or class teacher is ideally placed to organise the observation system for the setting and to co-ordinate the observations taken by all staff and to ensure that all areas of the curriculum are covered. There will also be occasions when further information about a child is required and then an observation should have a particular focus. This is likely to be the situation for children acquiring English as an additional language. Remember that all observations should have the name and age of the child together with the date the observation was taken. A short context paragraph is usually helpful so that when an observation is reread and analysed any important or relevant information is known. Write down exactly what is being observed without any interpretation or analysis. This will occur later. Different types of observation techniques are suited to different situations and information requirements.

- *Longitundal observations*. As the name suggests this is a collection of short, descriptive observations carried out over a period of time, perhaps over six months to one year. It can provide information about several aspects of development including progress in a child's home language and their new additional languages. It can be used to discuss the child's progress with parents and very often will provide them with reassurance as to the English language skills that have been developed over this period of time.

- *Free description observations*. This type of observation is probably the type most frequently carried out in nurseries. It is a record of events as they take place. In order to avoid spending a long period of time writing, it can be helpful to decide in advance what the particular focus is going to be. For example, during a small-group play activity can an emerging bilingual child express his needs and wishes using different types of communication skills? If after analysing the observation this proves to be the case, this is a very positive step to note. The observation may also reveal some tentative English language skill development perhaps with 'mine' or 'please' or 'thank you'. If a child is finding difficulty with communication then additional adult support needs to be planned.

■ *Checklists*. This method of observation is useful to quickly assess an area of development. It should not be used in isolation but preferably with other types of observation that provide a fuller picture of the child's achievements. Checklists do not have a holistic approach but are a useful tool. A checklist should identify what children can do rather than what they cannot do. The checklist has to be prepared in advance with criteria relevant to the area of development identified. The checklist on page 48 is an example of a checklist that a setting might have to help decide how well a particular child who is bilingual has settled into their nursery. The checklist covers all aspects of development but gives emphasis to the child being happy to communicate and play with other children and to join in with regular nursery activities. Staff add dated comments in the right-hand section and note if there are any associated photographs, observations or samples of the children's work which support their comments. Parents should be offered the opportunity to contribute examples of their children's achievements from home using photographs, and if required, with assistance from a bilingual member of staff.

■ *Language sampling*. The use of a tape recorder needs permission from the child's parents and can provide examples of a child's language development to keep for analysis and reference. The recording has to be set up in one particular place where the child is likely to be spending time in the same area, such as in a construction play area. The taped observation is best when it is backed up with a short written observation which provides the context and identifies the nature of the play and the participants.

Bilingual staff can observe children using their first language and the ways in which they switch from one language to another. Observation of children's first and additional languages will enable the full range of learning and understanding to take place. In some instances staff will observe the situations in which children will make their first tentative steps in English and after sharing this information make plans to build on this success. Some children will have a particular interest and want to learn associated vocabulary, look at books and sing songs connected with this topic, and other children may enjoy creative activities and start to talk about their drawings and pictures.

Discussion and analysis of the observations need to take place regularly so that a huge amount of information does not build up and the task becomes too big. Staff could take responsibility for a group of children and organise the review for their group of children, collecting views and deciding with other staff how the information will feed back into planning. Over a period of a term all the children should have had some observation and review.

Child's Name: Date of Observation: Observed by: Context:	Comment by Staff and Parents
1. Observes what other children are doing and copies their actions.	
2. Can express needs and wishes in their first language.	
3. Shows understanding through participation in play activities indoors and outdoors.	
4. Participates in routine nursery activities with adult support.	
5. Shows understanding by following simple instructions.	
6. Enjoys some dual-language stories read in their first language.	
7. Can use tape/IT facilities to listen to stories of their own choice.	
8. Asks questions from adults using their first language.	
9. Asks questions from other children using their first language.	
10. Initiates conversation using their first language.	
11. Carries out appropriate tasks of responsibility confidently.	
12. Uses greetings such as 'Hello', 'Goodbye' in English.	
13. Can repeat some words in English when supported by appropriate gestures and visual cues.	
14. Can name some everyday classroom objects in English when in an appropriate context.	
15. Can use one word responses appropriately and with increasing confidence.	

Guidlines for staff to review children's progress

When carrying out observation, staff need to remember that children need time to think before making a response which can take many forms, not only a verbal response. Written observations enable practitioners to make an assessment of progress or lack of progress and to identify the child's abilities and then plan to build on these or, in some cases, to plan for additional support.

Assessment as a celebration of children's achievements

Assessment that is evidenced based, that is, assessment derived from child observation enables professional judgements to be made on whether what has been planned with regard to children's learning has been effective. If the planning has been effective then practitioners make decisions on what the next steps should be for learning to progress. If, on the other hand, a judgement is made that planning has been ineffective then, after suitable discussion and reflection, further planning takes place. None of this can happen unless an assessment has been made. Assessment tools need to take into account cultural influences and language ability. Assessments taking place initially in the child's first language will give a fuller picture than those made using only English.

Formative assessment is based on observations taken as part of everyday nursery activity and can be used to inform planning on an ongoing basis. It is a very useful tool as it enables staff to really know the children and to plan for their individual learning needs. Summative assessment is also based on observation but is likely to happen at particular times such as at the end of the Early Years Foundation Stage or when a child transfers to a different setting.

The focus of any language assessment is to identify what the child can do and what actions are necessary for the individual child to make progress. Confidence needs to be built and successes celebrated. Language is part of children's communication strategies and nursery staff need to identify the communication that is taking place in a range of different situations and with different children and staff. All staff who come into contact with a particular child need to contribute to the assessment as they will observe the child from different perspectives. In this way assessment becomes collaborative. The teacher or key worker can co-ordinate the collection of observation material and lead the discussion about how the information gained from observation will be fed back into planning. Many settings keep observations and samples of the children's work in a portfolio. This is kept centrally and is available to staff, parents and children, and ideally should be set up before the home visit takes place. The purpose of the portfolio is to build up a clear picture of the child's progress in learning towards the stepping stones and the early learning goals. The entries will also contribute to the writing of the summative assessment. All staff need to be aware of how the portfolio will be organised, perhaps in chronological date order or in sections relating to the six areas of the Early Years Foundation Stage curriculum. Whatever system is chosen, it has to be manageable for staff in terms of collection of material. The information should be accessible to parents and should be available in the first language as well as in English. If there are no bilingual staff in the setting who can assist first-language entries in the portfolio, then an alternative strategy is to agree a time to discuss the portfolio with parents and to enlist the help of an interpreter from the local community or a bilingual member of staff from the language support unit. Staff will need to observe the setting's policies with regard to confidential and sensitive information and keep this detail in an appropriate place.

It is useful to give these portfolios a memorable name for the children such as 'My All About Me Book'. In this way the children identify with their portfolio, contribute to its content and from time to time look at it by themselves or with a member of staff and have pride in and can reflect on their learning. Parents should be asked if they wish to contribute to the portfolio, and children themselves will soon join in the collection of work of which they are very proud and may ask if a photograph can be taken of a model or some of their writing put into their special folder.

An 'All About Me' portfolio kept in a ring binder can contain:

- an introduction for parents which gives brief detail about the Early Years Foundation Stage curriculum

- the reason for compiling the portfolio and the uses to which the information will be put

- information about the child discussed during the home visit including languages spoken by the child and their parents

- observations made during nursery activities

- photographs which are relevant to the observations

- transcriptions from any language tape observations

- examples of children's use of first language communication

- samples of the children's work including photographs of role play in the imaginative play area, photographs of models, constructions and creative activities. When work and photographs are annotated with dates and comments these are helpful in building up a fuller picture of the child. Notes can include details of attitudes to learning such as being co-operative, showing perseverance and being fanatically interested in dinosaurs!

- contributions from parents using photographs of what the child has achieved at home. Parents could take photographs or talk with a bilingual member of staff who then makes an appropriate entry in the portfolio

- assessment of the children's achievements and the next steps for learning based on discussion and evaluation of observations.

Staff will need to discuss observations and the content of the portfolio and identify where the child needs additional support and how this will be provided. This can be further discussed at a planning meeting when resources are considered.

The *Foundation Stage Profile* is a more formal method of assessment which is based on the practitioner's observations and knowledge of the child. Practitioners should continue to use the *Foundation Stage Profile* handbook and profile. From September 2008 it will become the *Early Years Foundation Stage Profile*. The profile addresses three aspects of the achievements of children learning English as an additional language: 'development in the home language; development across the curriculum assessed through the home language; and development of English' (QCA/DfES, 2003a: 117).

The handbook also contains some extended scales for listening, speaking, reading and writing taken from 'A language in common: assessing English as an additional language' published by the Qualifications and Curriculum Authority – www. qca.org.uk. The document covers key points relating to the assessment of English as an additional language. The extended scales provide further guidance for practitioners as to what they may be able to identify in the early stages of English language development.

The first two steps in the extended scale for listening and speaking are especially relevant in the early stages of children acquiring English as an additional language, but practitioners should be aware that it might take some time for the children to reach these steps and that they need to enjoy many language experiences such as stories and songs before any anxiety about reaching these levels is expressed.

> *The extended scale for listening*
> *Step 1.* Pupils listen attentively for short bursts of time. They use non-verbal gestures to respond to greetings and questions about themselves, and they follow simple instructions based on the routines of the classroom.
> *Step 2.* Pupils understand simple conversational English. They listen and respond to the gist of general explanations by the teacher where language is supported by non-verbal cues, including illustrations.

> *The extended scale for speaking*
> *Step1.* Pupils echo words and expressions drawn from classroom routines and social interactions to communicate meaning. They express some basic needs, using single words or phrases in English.
> *Step 2.* Pupils copy talk that has been modelled. In their speech, they show some control of English word order and their pronunciation is generally intelligible. (QCA/DfES, 2003a: 119)

Children are unlikely to make progress at the same rate in all four language modes of listening, speaking, reading and writing. There may be initial success in listening activities prior to achievements in speaking, which will precede reading and writing progress. Some children will initially be happier to communicate in play situations or when taking part in outdoor activities, and may appear not to be communicating in group activities. However, it is important to remember that children experience a 'silent period' and although they may not be joining in the discussion they may be actively listening at story time and showing interest through facial expressions or by joining in the actions of a particular song such as 'Peter has one hammer'.

Past experiences, cultural and developmental factors may affect any assessment and should be taken into account. There are some 'prompts' in the *Foundation Stage Profile* handbook (QCA/DfES, 2003a: 105–11) which could be used by staff if some guidance is required as to what discussion topics to use as a basis for contributions by parents and children.

The *Foundation Stage Profile* document contains a space for notes relating to the child's progress in English as an additional language but in practice a more complete language record needs to be kept in the child's portfolio so that there is sufficient detail of the child's language achievements. The *Foundation Stage Profile* handbook offers guidance in what information relevant to achievements in other languages could be entered in the profile record, including:

- other languages that are understood by the child

- languages that are spoken by the child

- languages used to speak to parents, grandparents and siblings

- language experiences such as a knowledge of rhymes, stories and poems that are known by the child in the home language

- any future plans for the child to read and write in the home language.

The handbook gives guidance as to which of the assessment scales can be assessed through the children's home language, if support is available, and which of the assessment scales must be assessed in English.

Assessments across the areas of learning in the *Foundation Stage Profile* can be made through the home language as follows:

- all the scales in personal, social and emotional development

- all the scales in mathematical development

- all the scales in knowledge and understanding of the world, physical development and creative development

- the first three scale points (below the level of the early learning goals) in all the scales for communication, language and literacy.

Points 4–9 of the communication, language and literacy scale must be assessed in English. Where it has not been possible to access the child's full understanding through the child's first language, this should be recorded (QCA/DfES, 2003a: 118).

What learning can be assessed from an observation?

May (aged 2½) was playing on her own with a garage and a selection of brightly coloured cars. In addition to the cars there was one red bus in which six passengers could ride. Each car could have one passenger and the passengers depicted family members including mummy, daddy, granny and an uncle called Dom and an assortment of friends. She spent a considerable amount of time putting each car plus passenger in the garage lift and winching it up to the roof of the garage to place it on one of the coloured sections on the roof turntable. She provided her own running commentary throughout her play and sang the song 'The wheels on the bus go round and round'.

Physical development. Is able to use fine manipulative skills, hand–eye co-ordination to place and remove the passengers in the car and bus. Can use the winch to put the cars onto the garage roof and then the turntable handle to place the cars in a position of her choosing.

Cognitive development. Knows the names of the primary colours. Counts the cars on the roof top and the passengers on the bus. Has memorised all of the words of the song 'The wheels of the bus'. Uses imagination to make up a short story sequence for uncle Dom. Understands one-to-one correspondence allocating a passenger to a bus.

Language development. Uses prepositions on, in, up and down appropriately in their correct context. Adapts the words of the song to her actions such as getting the 'mummy' to chat to a 'friend' on the bus and saying 'mummies on the bus go chatter, chatter, chatter'. Happily takes on appropriate conversation of other characters such as 'Dom is going surfing'.

Emotional and social development. Plays happily on her own maintaining concentration and perseverance in placing the cars in their appropriate colour matching section of the roof turntable. When encountering some problems with the winching mechanism confidently asks for help from an adult then returns contentedly to continue with her play.

Planning the curriculum

Effective planning takes into consideration the children's interests and builds on their existing knowledge, skills and understanding. Good planning ensures that there are many opportunities for learning which cover all areas of the Early Years Foundation Stage curriculum, encourages children to have positive attitudes to their learning and offers a balance between adult-led and child-initiated activities. There should also be opportunity for play both inside and outside as both are valuable learning environments. The document *Planning for Learning in the Foundation Stage* provides detail for practitioners regarding long-term, medium-term and short-term plans and contains examples of how to write these plans. It identifies effective planning as a key factor in children's learning: 'Good planning is the key to making children's learning effective, exciting, varied and progressive' (QCA/DfES 2003b: 2).

Research conducted by Gillian Pugh identifies good planning practice as where planning uses as its basis children's thoughts, feelings, learning and development. It is essential that practitioners retain an element of flexibility in their planning and have the professional competence and confidence to seize unplanned opportunities to follow the children's lead when an unforeseen exciting or memorable event occurs. Plans do offer the opportunity to organise resources and give confidence to staff in knowing they are offering a balanced curriculum but they are not documents 'written in stone'.

Planning is effective and meets the learning needs of young children when:

- plans are informed by observations of the children

- plans include learning activities that build on what children know, understand and can do

- plans give priority to personal, social and emotional development

- curriculum content is offered at different levels to meet the differing needs of children

- curriculum activities are motivating and developmentally appropriate for the children

- plans acknowledge the importance of the learning process, not only the learning outcomes

- there is a balance between adult-led and child-initiated activities

- learning can take place both indoors and outdoors through first-hand experiences

- plans are regularly evaluated and reflected on to meet the needs and interests of the children

- plans identify what the next steps are for individual children, for example, practise, consolidate and move on

- children are given opportunities to be active learners

- children are offered opportunities to make responsible, informed choices and decisions

- children are supported to become autonomous learners

- plans identify how staff will be deployed to support and extend the children's learning

- staff know that plans can be adapted as they listen to and observe children

- staff have the time and opportunity to be involved in the children's play

- all staff are involved in planning so that they can contribute different ideas and perspectives

- staff share the plans with parents so that they can support their children's learning

- staff organise the environment so that learning spaces 'work' for the benefit of children

- resources are organised so that they can be independently accessed by the children.

Planning to meet the needs of children learning English as an additional language should be embedded in the planning for the whole group of children. There needs to be continuity and progression for the children so that they can use their first language and in addition gain English language skills.

Bilingual learning is promoted when planning:

- builds on and values the child's previous experiences

- enables the child's first language to be supported during everyday activities

- enables children to be part of a small group involved in routine nursery activities

- offers opportunity for one-to-one interaction between the child and a member of staff

- offers children opportunities for communicating in different ways, but especially in talking

- recognises that listening and being listened to is a key part of language learning

- acknowledges that first-hand experiences are the foundation for language learning

- offers play opportunities as the context for language learning

- enables adult and peers to model English language supported by visual material

- includes the use of resources that are familiar to children

- includes the use of dual-language texts for use by all of the children

- ensures that parents are kept fully informed of their children's learning and progress

- deploys bilingual staff in a supportive role to share with other staff the child's feelings and experiences.

Summary: key principles for effective planning

- Observation and assessment are part of the planning cycle.

- Effective observation enables staff to know their children's interest and learning styles.

- Assessment celebrates what children can do rather than what they cannot do.

- Assessment tools need to be appropriate for a child's current experiences.

- Planning needs to be flexible in order to respond to children's interests.

CHAPTER 5

A curriculum for the early years

This chapter considers aspects of the curriculum for the early years used in various settings including nursery schools, pre-schools, day nurseries, children's centres and in the home setting with childminders, together with the way in which children learn through play and the crucial role that staff have in helping children learn through well planned and resourced play-based activities.

- The Early Years Foundation Stage curriculum for children from birth to 5 years.
- Play as part of the early years curriculum
- Reflective practice
- Using curriculum activities to support learning English as an additional language.

The Early Years Foundation Stage is based on four principles which support the care, learning and development for all young children from birth until the end of the academic year in which the child has their fifth birthday. These four principles are:

A Unique Child

Positive Relationships

Enabling Environments

Learning and Development.

These four themes provide the context in which practitioners plan and support all the aspects of children's development and learning. Each of these four themes is organised into four 'commitments' which describe how the principles can be put into practice.

A Unique Child: Child Development, Inclusive Practice, Keeping Safe and Health and Well-being.

Positive Relationships: Respecting Each Other, Parents as Partners, Supporting Learning and the Key Person.

Enabling Environments: Observation, Assessment and Planning, Supporting Every Child, The Learning Environment and the Wider Context

Learning and Development: Play and Exploration, Active Learning, Creativity and Thinking and Areas of Learning and Development.

The Early Years Foundation Stage brings together and takes forward the principles and the approach previously found in the *Curriculum Guidance for the Foundation Stage*, the *Birth to Three Matters* framework and the National Standards for Under-8s Daycare and Childminding.

Practioners who have worked with these frameworks will find some elements of familiarity both in the format and the content. Resources available to practioners and providers include the Statutory Framework, the Practice Guidance for the Early Years Foundation Stage and the Principles into Practice cards. These cards, similar to those included with the Birth to Three Matters framework, carry links to the Key Elements of Effective Practice (KEEP) which is used as an evaluation tool for practioners to reflect on their practice and their provision for young children and their families.

The Principle into Practice cards highlight links to the *Every Child Matters* agenda which focuses on bringing together services to support children and families. The effective use of the Early Years Foundation Stage will enable practioners to meet the five outcomes of the framework.

In addition to this supportive material there is also a CD ROM which contains background information on the framework together with detail on the Early Years Profile and registration and inspection relevant to the framework requirements. Practioners will also be able to find information and video clips on effective practice, research and resources which can be used to support further professional development as well as their own practice.

There are some important messages contained in this framework that have value for practioners. There is a strong emphasis on developmentally appropriate practice and clear expectations for working with young bilingual children. In the Principles into Practice card the theme 'Enabling Environment' related to Communication, Language and Literacy gives guidance to practitioners:

'Show particular awareness of, and sensitivity to, the needs of children learning English as an additional language. Use their home language when appropriate and ensure close teamwork between practitioners, parents and bilingual workers so that the children's developing use of English and other languages support each other.'

This guidance is centred on the child's needs based on practitioner observation rather than a pre-planned adult agenda.

As part of forward planning, the nursery practitioners arranged for a bilingual member of staff to make a recording of the story *A Dark, Dark, Tale* by Ruth Brown translated into chinese by Sylvia Denham and published in dual-language form by Mantra. During the half-term topic on animals, all the children enjoyed the spooky story which followed a black cat through a myriad of adventures which started on a dark, dark moor through a dark, dark hall and finally into a corner where there was a dark, dark box which contained … a mouse complete with huge ears and wide staring eyes. The children enjoyed pretending to be very frightened as they gazed intently at the evocative illustrations. Roland was able to read and listen to his own story in Chinese and with all the other children learn about traditional beginnings for stories such as 'Once upon a time', join in the repetition and look for the rocking horse, the rabbits and the animals

The Early Years Foundation Stage framework for children aged three to five years

This framework becomes mandatory for early years settings in September 2008 but many settings have chosen to implement the framework before this date. The Childcare Act 2006 provides for the Early Years Foundation Stage and sets out three elements: the early learning goals, the educational programme and the assessment arrangements. All early years providers must by law deliver the framework from September 2008 regardless of the type of setting, their size, or the funding of the setting. Parents will choose from a variety of settings according to their need and the needs of their children. These settings will include nurseries, nursery schools, pre-schools, children's centres and in the home setting with child minders. Some children attend more than one type of setting and ideally the staff in the settings need to work together and with the parents so that there is a seamless transition for the children from one setting to another.

The Early Years Foundation Stage guidance related to 'The Enabling Environment and the Wider Context' asks practitioners to reflect on their practice with regard to having a policy for transition and continuity which is shared with everyone involved both in and beyond the setting.

Some children will leave their nursery school with their childminder and then spend a few hours in this new setting. The choice of settings and their different approaches and hours of operating can be quite bewildering for parents newly arrived in the country. Children's Information Centres are a helpful source of information. Children may also be confused and feel unsettled and need particular support from key practitioners to experience a sense of stability and security. In thinking how to successfully manage these situations it is helpful to think how it must be like from the child's perspective. Bilingual staff or the use of interpreters is vital to ensure that there is as much understanding as possible on the part of parents and children. It is insufficient to put in this support just in the beginning as 'a one off' situation as parents do not always know what questions to ask or what concerns they or their children might have and these only become apparent as time goes on and then support is still needed. In addition to information about the organisation and staff of a particular setting, parents may appreciate an explanation of the structure of the foundation stage curriculum and the place of play in their children's learning and how play will support the acquisition of English as an additional language.

In the *Practice Guidance for the Early Years Foundation Stage* six key issues are identified which when appropriately implemented are likely to result in the successful delivery of the framework and in so doing meet children's needs.

Meeting the diverse needs of children

Partnership working

Flexible provision

Play

Quality improvement

Transition, continuity and coherence

(DfES, 2007: 6–10)

There is guidance for practioners in promoting and developing play to underpin all development and learning for young children. This indicates a requirement for a very active role on the part of early years staff to promote play and learning when working with children. The role of staff is one of empowerment and nurture so that children have positive attitudes to learning. Children not only benefit from acquiring knowledge but also the skills which will enable them to take responsibility for their own learning and be curious and inquisitive about the world around them. Children learning English as an additional language frequently have experiences that give them a broader perspective and in time ones that they willingly share with their peers and with staff.

In recent times there has been a better understanding of the importance of quality early years care and education for very young children and with this improved understanding has come additional funding and a host of new initiatives, including the curriculum frameworks for children. However, the success of the early years curriculum frameworks, as seen in the children's learning and development, rests with appropriately qualified and experienced practitioners who have the responsibility for the teaching and learning within their setting. There can be the most modern of buildings with good quality, abundant resources but the key factor in offering children excellent experiences will be the staff.

When practitioners have sound professional expertise which includes high-level qualifications and extensive experience, they can lead teams to deliver the best for children. Some practitioners find the thought of working in early years settings very daunting as they are busy, ever-changing environments which can be physically and mentally exhausting. It is, however, the most rewarding of experiences in seeing the children flourish, gain in independence and develop their own unique characters. Increasingly, all practitioners will need the skills, knowledge and understanding of how emerging bilingual children can best be supported to access the early years curriculum as the number of children entering nurseries from different language backgrounds increases. Young bilingual children are not only learning a new language but they need this new language in order to be able to benefit from the curriculum. This is in addition to maintaining their skills in their first language. All this is quite a challenge not only for the children but also for staff! The website, www.mantralingua.com, from the UK publishing house has excellent literacy resources to support English and many first languages. It publishes a host of best-selling children's books in many languages in addition to posters and interactive CD-ROMs.

Different aspects of the curriculum make different demands on children learning English as an additional language. They need the opportunity to have respite from very challenging activities and to be able to express themselves and communicate in easier ways, perhaps through physical and creative activities. All children experience the ebb and flow which is part of every early years settings and can pace themselves if there are suitable activities and environments from which they can choose.

The Early Years Foundation Stage curriculum is an appropriate framework for embedding the teaching and learning of English as an additional language when staff are clear about what they want the children to learn and how this can best be achieved for individual children. In planning for bilingual children it is preferable to offer many play-based activities, to follow the interests of the children as seen in observation, for any tasks set to be clearly explained, purposeful and active, to offer appropriate peer and staff support, and to remember to praise not only achieved outcomes, if any, but also the processes involved and the effort made.

The organisation of the learning environment both indoors and outdoors can be instrumental in enabling bilingual learners to make progress. An environment which promotes learning is organised to:

- be safe for all children

- be accessible to all children and parents and where possible have ramps for wheel chair access

- be predictable for children so that they know the places where particular activities will happen

- have resources labelled in the children's languages or use common symbols

- have resources easily accessible to children to encourage independent learning

- have resources which are relevant and familiar to the children's cultures

- have resources that can be used by children with special educational needs

- have sufficient resources to enable the curriculum to be offered at different levels

- have suitable storage areas so that children can care for equipment and themselves take appropriate responsibility for tidying up

- have a selection of resources that are available on a daily basis which are then supplemented to extend learning and to respond to children's observed interests

- have some protected spaces for children who are building with blocks or making constructions

- have display areas for children's work including constructions, sculptures and photographs of them playing, dancing and enjoying music

- have a quiet area for children playing or looking at books by themselves

- have a quiet area for one-to-one discussions

- have a quiet area to listen to taped first-language stories

- have a comfy area to snuggle down and rest, look at books or just to think quietly

- have the outdoor area staffed to be available to children for as much of the day as possible

- have the outdoor area resourced for a range of learning opportunities including physical, creative and language activities

- have sufficiently large spaces for children to run, jump and be physically creative.

Staff directly influence the curriculum by the way in which they plan the layout of the environment. In so doing they need to have high expectations of all the children and promote independence and self-esteem. Within the curriculum framework staff can differentiate to meet the needs of all children through the level of specific support offered and through what Bruce (2005: 253) describes as 'double provision'. This is where there are sufficient resources that enable children to use the materials at starting points relevant to their individual levels of development. Children are able to extend their own learning when there are enough relevant resources available to them. When staff know each child well through regular observation, it enables them to plan appropriately for differentiation and to meet individual needs including those of children with disability and those who are more able. The website from the DfES provides information about the English as an additional language activities developed within the Primary National Strategy framework – www.standards.dfes.gov.uk.

The Primary Framework for Literacy and Mathematics and the Early Years Foundation Stage have been developed alongside each other. They help practitioners to see how the six areas of the Foundation Stage curriculum link to literary and mathematics in Key Stage 1 of the National Curriculum.

The Every Child Matters – Change for Children is a far reaching programme that underpins all recent early years legislation. It has as its objective the wish to improve outcomes for young people, children and their families. The Children Act 2004 provided the legislative framework for the far-reaching reform programme. It is a government-funded framework to ensure that children and young people from birth to 19 years have the necessary support to achieve the five outcomes that have been identified as the key to well-being in childhood and in later life. These outcomes are:

■ being healthy

■ staying safe

■ enjoying and achieving

■ making a positive contribution

■ achieving economic well-being.

A key objective of the programme is 'to close the gap in outcomes between disadvantaged children and their peers'. Particularly relevant to emerging bilingual children are the outcomes for 'Enjoying and achieving' which are described as being 'ready for school and attending and enjoying school'. Many children newly arriving in this country will find some of the services offered through the Every Child Matters programme very helpful in enabling them to settle into their new life and feel ready to learn.

The National Services Framework for Children, Young People and Maternity Services is a 10-year programme designed to achieve sustained improvement in children's health and well-being and an integral part of the Every Child Matters programme aiming to support families from pregnancy onwards. Where there is 'joined up' provision encompassing health care, childcare and education and family support it should enable the children of all newly arriving families and those struggling with the demands of English as an additional language to have the best possible start in life. All parents will benefit from an integrated approach where practitioners from a range of services work together sharing professional information so that the five key outcomes are achieved. Many families are already receiving support through the Sure Start children's centres, which offer an integrated approach. These centres are thought to be crucial in achieving the outcomes of the Every Child Matters framework. The centres are managed through partnerships that reflect local need and diversity, and have a management structure that should include the users of the services themselves. With effective support, parents who have children learning English as an additional language can make a contribution that will ensure that the services remain responsive to local need.

Play as part of the early years curriculum

The *Practice Guidance for the Early Years Foundation Stage* places strong emphasis on the importance of play in the early years curriculum: In playing, children behave in different ways: 'sometimes their play will be boisterous, sometimes they will describe and discuss what they are doing, and sometimes they will be quiet and reflective as they play' DfES (2007: 7). Children who are emerging bilinguals also find play reassuring as they sort out their new world with the many varied and challenging experiences they are having. The debate about play in the early years curriculum has always been vigorous. Early years practitioners know without a doubt that play must have a place in the curriculum but sometimes find it difficult to be convincing advocates for this approach when in discussion with parents and other professionals. Play provides for the children's control of their learning experiences, a degree of familiarity in their fast-changing world, and reassurance and security. It offers first-hand experiences on which they can extend their learning and understanding. However, there is also a place for direct teaching, especially when a child is becoming frustrated and cannot carry out a task which could be completed with a helping hand from a sensitive adult. When this 'helping hand' shows how to achieve the task in small, easy steps rather than just 'doing it' for the child it is quite likely that this new skill will be learnt and quickly used.

During play, children are active learners, use their senses to explore and experiment, have many first-hand experiences with natural materials and then re-present these experiences through writing, drawing, modelling, dancing and other creative activities. In this way they take ownership of their learning and enjoy thinking back about their experiences and look forward to other experiences. Initially, some children will find it more difficult to join in play activities and will watch as interested observers. They may, however, be listening closely and tuning in to their new language while also taking the opportunity to work out the 'rules' of any game and the behaviours that are needed. In so doing they are building confidence and getting ready for their first steps in joining the play of their peers. These first steps may well involve the children using their first language and this should be encouraged. Children will comment on their play, talk themselves through situations, ask questions and build on their existing first-language skills. They talk to themselves to organise their thinking and their activities and to think through what it is they want to do. In time they will use these first-language skills and transfer them to their emerging English language skills. As they take part in play they will become part of their new environment, build friendships and self-esteem and gradually relax into their learning. Bruce and Meggit state that 'free flow play helps children to use what they know and apply it to new situations in a safe, secure context of playing' (2005: 229).

During play, children who are new to the setting will be learning from their peers in a reassuring environment. They will hear everyday English phrases modelled for them by children with whom they are playing. Young children do not need to learn English through meaningless vocabulary lists, they need to acquire their English language skills in a meaningful context. Because of the context they can make sense of what they are hearing and try it out when ready. They feel part of the group and are not being isolated or made to feel different. Skilled practitioners need to observe the children's play and to note the children's interests and their readiness to communicate in English. At this point the children need plenty of support and opportunities to repeat and practise new phrases. If the imaginative play area is organised as a shop the children will hear greetings and phrases such as 'Good morning', 'Hello' and 'What do you want?', 'What would you like?', 'Goodbye'. These everyday phrases can be used on a daily basis when welcoming and working with the children in the classroom. Repetition in a relevant context offers children chances to consolidate their learning and feel proud of their achievements. The imaginative play area also provides the opportunity to include culturally relevant resources that can be helpful to children learning about their new culture and on other occasions to offer all children the motivation to learn about cultures different from their own.

Play does not necessarily have an outcome; it is the processes of play which are beneficial and provide the learning experience. If practitioners understand the importance of play in the children's learning they will make every effort to organise the environment and the nursery day so that play is protected and valued. Play is at the heart of a developmentally appropriate curriculum.

Bruce (2005: 230) offers 12 features of play which 'help adults to recognise and cultivate free flow play of quality'. She describes free-flow play as 'helping children to use what they know and apply it to new situations in a safe, secure context of playing'. The 12 features of play are:

1. Using first-hand experiences

2. Making up rules

3. Making props

4. Choosing to play

5. Rehearsing the future

6. Pretending

7. Playing alone

8. Playing together

9. Having a personal agenda

10. Being deeply involved

11. Trying out recent learning

12. Co-ordinating ideas, feelings and relationships for the free-flow play.

These 12 features can be used to asses and evaluate play. Bruce suggests that when perhaps seven or more features are observed, then children are likely to be involved in quality play. If staff working with children learning English as an additional language can identify these features as they carry out child observations, then it is likely that the children are having beneficial play experiences on which language foundations can be built. Children are unable to develop their language and engage in meaningful conversation if they have had no experiences to share and discuss.

In each of the six areas of learning forming part of the Early Years Foundation Stage framework there is guidance for the practitioner as to the 'building blocks' that children may work towards before achieving the relevant early learning goal. These 'building blocks' can be found under the heading of Development Matters and are linked to the child's chronological age. The early learning goals are grouped under the same heading written in bold type.

> Reina was just over 3 years of age when she came from Japan to England with her mother to attend the nursery on a daily basis. As part of their planning for the summer term the staff decided they would encourage the children to find out more about Japan and how Japanese children and their parents celebrate the festival of 'Shichi-go-san'. This national holiday celebrates the health and happiness of children aged 7, 5 and 3 which is the meaning of shichi-go-san. Reina felt very proud when her mother came to the nursery and showed all the children the photographs of her family celebrating the festival when the children dressed in their best clothes and visited the temple. The nursery children were fascinated by the photographs in which some of Reina's family were wearing traditional kimonos and they wanted to know more about Japan. Over the next few weeks the nursery staff welcomed Reina's mother to the nursery to demonstrate her origami skills. She showed the children the special origami paper which had beautiful patterns on one side. The children used the paper to make some small fans which they had seen in some of the festival photographs.

Some of the knowledge and understanding of the world 'development matters' criteria were identified by staff in their planning for the celebration of 'Shichi-go-san' including:

- 'Show interest in the lives of people familiar to them.'

- 'Remember and talk about significant events in their own experience'.

Reina felt immensely proud that the staff and other children were interested in her experiences and felt especially pleased when her mother visited the nursery. Some of the stepping stones for personal, social and emotional development were met from Reina's perspective including:

- Talk freely about their home and community (with the support of her mother)

- Have a sense of personal identity (QCA/DfES, 2000).

The staff were pleased to have the support of Reina's mother and she enjoyed getting to know them better. The topic developed into directions that had not initially been planned for but with help the staff were able to follow the children's lead and find suitable resources for their imaginative role play.

Reflective practice

It is important for staff to be able to take some time away from the busy nursery day to reflect on and evaluate the curriculum activities offered to the children. This is easier in some settings than in others, but how are staff to know if the children are making progress with their learning if evaluation does not take place? Reflection is an effective tool for improving chosen aspects of early years care, and education and is one of the hallmarks of a profession. Through reflection, personal and professional strengths are identified together with gaps in knowledge and areas of practice requiring further support. It is also a means by which success is identified and celebrated. Too often practitioners spend a great deal of time concentrating on practice which needs to be improved at the expense of celebrating good and effective practice. In this way practitioners value themselves and their work.

Reflective activity requires honest discussion between all staff starting with an open mind and a willingness to look at practices that have been in place for a long time and to consider if there might be better ways of doing things or changes that could be made in the light of research findings, practical experiences or the strengths that new staff may have brought to the setting. Well-founded and evidence-based changes enable staff to 'recharge' their batteries and enjoy approaching a regularly planned topic from a different perspective. An enthusiastic approach from staff benefits the children too!

Effective reflection takes place within the framework of a supportive team environment. This means that ideas and concerns are shared, and suggested ways of improvement are tested through robust discussion before any implementation. It is a way of considering if what is said to happen in policies or other documents actually does happen and if necessary to ask, if not, why not? The consequences of any changes have to be thought through, with implications for children, parents and staff considered. When any agreed changes are put in practice they need to be monitored and then evaluated. Very often a person who is not directly involved with the proposed changes can work with staff to act as a 'critical friend' who listens, raises questions, looks at the wider view, tests hypotheses and supports change. Through engaging in reflective activity, staff can gain confidence in their professional skills and are able to give well-founded explanations to parents and other professionals as to why they do what they do. They become proactive in resolving any difficulties, take responsibility for improvement and feel empowered while doing so. When taking part in reflective activities there is a heightened awareness of practice as though the practitioner is taking a step away from the busy nursery activities and is observing patterns of behaviour, similarities and differences in children's responses or successful interactions which can often be used to answer some of the concerns that have been raised by staff. After a period of reflection the way in which any changes will be made needs to be discussed.

Research conducted by the *Principles into Practice* team (Blenkin and Kelly, 1997) indicated that the main factor in improving the quality of provision offered to young children and their families lies with the practitioners themselves. For this reason early childhood staff need to become reflective practitioners and engage in small-scale research in their own setting. Blenkin and Kelly (1997: 92) commended the process of action research:

> It is critical, self evaluative inquiry that enables practitioners to consider the context of their practice. While conducting action research, practitioners are called to question particular

aspects of their practice, to articulate the underlying values and assumptions which inform and influence that practice, and to consider the effectiveness of their professional actions and judgements, especially in the light of the impact these have on the children with whom they work.

If the staff research, discussion and reflection, together with any changes to be tested, are documented, this is very helpful for future planning and research and it may save time as repetitive discussion and revisiting 'old ground' is avoided. Documenting research activity is also the starting point for sharing the research experience and the information gained from it. A journal or diary with regular entries relevant to the learning that has taken place by the members of the research team is a good basis for improving practice. Entries can include comment on:

- the context of the activity or the reading or event on which the reflection is to take place

- a brief description of the chosen 'critical' activity or event

- an exploration or 'thinking aloud' of the personal or professional significance

- a comment on the insight or learning that has been gained from the exploration

- a note about how this learning will link to the children's learning

- an outline of the team's collective thoughts about how practice could be improved

- a note about the resource implications

- a note about the possible implications for other members of staff and parents

- an outline of the future plan of action

- a note of the arrangements for the evaluation and professional discussion related to any changes.

One area for reflection can be to look at the curriculum from the point of view of a child learning English as an additional language. Prompts for focused reflection on English language development are helpful:

- Is the nursery policy to promote the children's first language implemented?

- Is there an agreed strategy for bilingual staff to interact with children in routine nursery activities?

- Is there appropriate bilingual support in place to assist parents and children?

- Do all staff have high expectations for children learning English as an additional language?

■ Are all staff clear about their role in effectively and appropriately supporting bilingual children?

■ Are staff aware of their influence as language role models?

■ Are there sufficient, relevant, good quality resources to support curriculum activities and provide familiar links with the children's own culture?

■ Does the book corner contain attractive, meaningful dual-language texts accessible to all children?

■ Has the agreed schedule for child observations taken place?

■ Has the information gained from the evaluation of the observation been shared with all staff and fed back into planning?

■ Have activities been planned to have a language focus to meet the needs of the children?

■ When planning curriculum activities, do staff ask themselves what kind of language might evolve for the activity?

■ When a specific language need has been identified, do staff plan ways of meeting this need?

■ Is the level of language used by staff appropriate for the attainment level of the individual child?

■ How does evaluation of planning for additional language development take place?

■ Which member of staff is responsible for this evaluation?

■ What happens to the information gained from the evaluation?

■ Are there sufficient opportunities for emerging bilingual children to have one-to-one interactions?

■ Are there opportunities to have conversations that are specifically directed at the children's observed interests?

■ Is the child's language development in both first language and English making progress?

There are other more general areas for small-scale research which will benefit all the children in the setting and over time will indicate how well settled the children new to English are. Children who are developing their skills as autonomous learners will have sufficient confidence to learn new language skills and be willing to try out new things, although this process can take place over a sustained period of time. The gradual development of young children as autonomous learners can be observed through certain characteristics. Children who are confident autonomous learners will be able to:

- act independently

- confidently choose activities

- initiate conversations

- try things out

- take appropriate risks in their learning

- understand that making mistakes is part of learning

- take decisions

- explore and carry out their own creative ideas

- invent their own play ideas

- feel proud of their new skills and knowledge

- work with other children as part of a team.

Practitioners who discuss and agree their own framework to observe autonomous learning have then formed their own research team and know that they 'own' the process and the analysis and reflection, together with any changes to practice which may follow. This is not to say that the team will always have the same view or agree with all of the research findings, but the honest discussion and awareness of different viewpoints is very healthy and has benefits. A similar research approach can then be applied to other aspects of practice which the staff decide may benefit from investigation. If the team is composed of different members of staff, this then becomes part of professional development as analytical, reflective, communication and team-building skills are developed. Reflective skills can also be developed through reading, professional discussion and visiting other settings, as well as attending external training or undertaking higher-level qualifications.

Reflective practice enables practitioners to continue with their learning, develop their professional competencies and enjoy new experiences. It is one of the most powerful tools for bringing about innovation and improvement.

Using curriculum activities to support learning English as an additional language

In Chapters 6 to 11 there are further details on each of the curriculum areas together with a variety of practical activities linked to each of the six areas. Although in each of these activities there is a focus on language, all the activities will promote other areas of the children's development. The topic web chart (see pp. x–xii) enables practitioners to see at a glance in which chapters there are activities connected with specific areas of learning or topics. Some vocabulary is listed as a key aspect of the activity, but it is essential to remember that children need the context for the vocabulary and will learn sentences and phrases in their entirety, not just as single words. The activities lend themselves to working with children in small groups, with children who have English as their first language as well as emerging bilingual children. They are examples of everyday early years activities so that all the children can be included, with a particular language focus for some children. The activities should be planned to be as interactive as possible and may well last for a week or longer as the children need time for skill development. It is beneficial for the children to revisit topics so that they build confidence and have opportunities to consolidate their learning. Other factors to be considered when planning and implementing the activities in Chapters 6 to 11 include:

- ensuring that all planning takes into account the need for staff support for the emerging bilingual children taking part in the activity

- bilingual staff support is beneficial prior to an activity to explain the concepts and sometimes at the start to build the children's confidence

- planning the groupings of children of varied language backgrounds so that all of their language needs are met and, if possible, provide role models for children learning English as an additional language

- planning the activities to be part of the everyday nursery curriculum using visual prompts whenever possible

- ensuring that the children carry out as much of the activity themselves as is possible

- starting each topic from what the children already know and can do, and then building on this

- the need for staff to scaffold the activity and to add relevant comment to the children's work

- the need for staff to continue building language skills even when there is no apparent response from the children

- valuing all the responses from the children including a few words in English and first-language contributions, gestures, movement or other responses such as making a model or a drawing

- ensuring that all resources used are inclusive for children who have additional learning needs as well as those learning English as an additional language.

Summary: a curriculum for the early years

■ The Early Years Foundation Stage framework emphasises the need for developmentally appropriate practice for children aged from birth to 5 years of age.

■ Practitioners need to plan for a smooth transition for children from each of their settings and to keep parents and colleagues informed.

■ Staff need to have an active approach in promoting children's language development within curriculum activities.

■ Well-planned play is an entitlement for all children.

■ Reflection is one of the key ways of improving practice.

■ Everyday nursery activities can support the development of language skills.

CHAPTER 6
Practical activities for personal, social and emotional development

This chapter considers how the early years practitioner can plan and resource activities which promote personal, emotional and social development. The development of personal, social and emotional skills is a priority for early years practitioners. When these skills are successfully promoted they form the foundation for achievement in all other areas of learning. Much of the nursery day is centred on activities which promote self-esteem and independence such as having milk and water freely available to the children so that they can take responsibility for choosing when to have it, pouring it carefully into a mug and then perhaps having a sociable time with their friends while they sit and enjoy their drink. The organisation of the play and learning environment so that children can access materials is another way of building self-worth and autonomy. Small-group times are excellent for building confidence and a positive sense of self. During the nursery day, children need to have opportunities to build their self-confidence, to acquire positive attitudes to learning and to take appropriate risks within a safe and supportive learning environment. Appointing a 'buddy' for the new arrival has benefits for both children.

On Izzy's first day in her reception class she knew that Hannah would be her special friend and look after her in the classroom and also in the playground. Izzy had recently arrived with her family from Morocco and knew few English words. She had visited the school the previous day to meet her teacher, to look round the school and to be introduced to Hannah. Izzy hesitantly came into the classroom with her grandfather and immediately looked for Hannah who smiled and suggested that she sit beside her on the carpet. During the day Hannah stayed with Izzy who carefully looked to see what Hannah was doing and tried to do likewise. In this way she was able to join in with most of the activities and felt she was like the other children. Hannah benefited from the increased responsibility and enjoyed being a leader which was a role new to her. She also felt able to help Izzy join in the playground activities of two of her other friends and the four girls played co-operatively.

It is important to give support to the children who are endeavouring to make their initial, tentative contributions in their first language, in English or, more frequently, in both languages. Supporting their first language enables them to settle, feel less anxious and to begin to participate and contribute. Their contributions can be verbal, through gesture, through the use of symbols or a mixture of all types of communication. All efforts in communicating should be praised and rewarded with whatever reward system is in use by the setting, for instance with stickers, a warm smile or celebrating the achievement

(Continued)

(Continued)

with a parent or carer. Within this area of learning the children have opportunities to respect themselves, their home and their new culture and that of the other children. They are also forming relationships and friendships and developing an enthusiastic approach to their learning. All these dispositions can be developed within everyday learning activities, which at the same time promote language skills.

Practical suggestions for activities which support the development of personal, social and emotional skills follow.

- All about me
- My family
- My day at nursery
- My home
- See what I can do!
- Feelings
- People who help us
- Keeping safe.

All about me

 ## Activity name: All about me

Objectives

To teach children the vocabulary for different parts of the body.

To begin to teach children to recognise small numbers of objects without counting.

To learn how to take turns and share within a small group.

To practise counting up to six.

Materials and preparation

Card and paper fasteners to make a large puppet-type figure. Photographs of children running, jumping, skipping and playing other games. Copies of the songs 'Head, shoulders, knees and toes' and 'One finger, one thumb, one arm, one leg, keep moving' if these songs are new to you. Materials for the activity based on the 'Beetle drive' game – large dice and simply drawn cardboard body parts.

What to do

1. Introduce the song 'Head, shoulders, knees and toes' with the relevant actions.

2. Encourage the children to join in with the actions.

3. Repeat the song several times without leaving the usual gaps in the song.

4. Recap the important vocabulary relevant to the different parts of the body.

5. Ask the children 'Where's your head?', 'Where are your shoulders?' encouraging them to point to the appropriate place. Continue with the rest of the body. Use the photographs to see body parts in action!

6. Repeat the song a little more slowly giving the children the opportunity to join in.

7. As a group activity, work with the children to make a large-size jointed figure with limbs fixed to the body with paper fasteners. The limbs can be jointed at the knee and elbow. Refer to the appropriate parts of the body.

8. Discuss with the children a suitable name for the figure, for example, Bob.

9. Using simple body part labels, ask the children to place the label on the correct body part saying the word as they do so. 'Can you find Bob's head?' Model the reply, 'Here's Bob's head'.

10. Bob can then become a class mobile and used for revision of body parts!

Extension activities

1. Introduce the second song 'One finger, one thumb, one arm, one leg'.

2. Organise another activity based on the 'Beetle drive' game. This will help with the recognition of small numbers of objects without counting. Some children may need some initial support with this.

3. Use the large puppet-like figure, Bob, as a model for this game. If possible help the children to make their own small puppet figure for the game.

4. Make sure that each child has a whole figure with the correct numbers of body parts.

5. As a group, each child takes it in turn to roll the dice and then to pick up the relevant body part. Encourage each child to either count the dots on the dice and say the number or to say 'That's a six' if this can be done without counting.

6. Collect the body parts to make a person, with each child saying the name of the body part appropriately. Explain to the children that the body must be collected before the head and then the other body parts. Encourage them to think why this is the case! A body outline which mirrors 'Bob' will help the children to place the collected body parts in the correct places.

    1 = body

    2 = head

3 = 2 legs

4 = 2 arms

5 = face (eyes, nose and mouth)

6 = 2 ears

7. Remember to give praise when any language contribution takes place such as numbers are correctly counted or recognised, body parts are correctly named or when turns are taken fairly.

Key vocabulary
Head, shoulders, knees, toes, eyes, ears, mouth, nose, finger, thumb, arm, leg, number names 1 to 6.

Links with Early Years Foundation Stage curriculum for personal, social and emotional development
Seek and delight in new experiences. Show confidence in linking up with others for support and guidance. Have a sense of personal identity.

My family

 Activity name: My family

Objectives

To discuss with children how families are composed of different people.

To introduce the names of different family members.

To use positional language in context.

Materials and preparation
Books relating to families. Photographs of family members. Large sheets of paper and drawing and writing materials. *Let's look at families* by Barbara Hunter, published by Heinemann. *When Grandma came* by Jill Paton Walsh and Sophie Williams published by Puffin Books.

What to do

1. Introduce the topic by reading a suitable book such as *When Grandma came*.

2. Discuss with the children the activities that they enjoy with their own family, being sensitive to children who may be experiencing difficult family circumstances such as bereavement, separation or divorce.

3. Using a large sheet of paper, draw a simple family tree showing three generations, that is, grandparents, parents and children. Encourage the children to draw their family members, taking it in turn to do the drawings.

4. Remember to accompany the drawing with repetition of the names of the family members. Children will probably point out that they use different names for family members, such as 'granny' or 'grandma'. This is an opportunity to talk with the children about how families are different but can also be similar in that they also enjoy the same activities such as going to the beach or to the park. In some cultures there are different names for the paternal and maternal grandparents.

5. When the family photographs have been brought into school, talk generally about the family members making sure to use a photograph from each child's family as part of the discussion.

6. Model the phrase, 'This is my mummy' in an answer to the question, 'Who's this'?

7. This should be followed by a short discussion about the family member with contributions from the children.

8. Draw another family tree for each child and encourage the child to place the photographs in the correct place accompanied by 'This is my daddy' and so on. If photographs are not available, use the children's drawings of their family members.

Extension activities

1. Include members of the extended family such as uncle, aunt and cousin and look at these relationships on the family tree.

2. Use positional language such as 'next to' or 'underneath' correctly as the children place their photographs or drawings on the family tree.

Key vocabulary

Mummy, daddy, grandma, granddad, brother, sister, aunt, uncle, cousin, under, over, above, beside, next to, near to.

Links with the Early Years Foundation Stage curriculum for personal, social and emotional development

Talk freely about their home and community. Enjoy joining in with family customs and routines. Have a sense of personal identity. Show a strong sense of self as a member of different communities, such as their family or setting. Make connections between different parts of their life experience.

My day at nursery

 Activity name: My day at nursery

Objectives

To offer reassurance to children through being able to predict nursery activities.

To discuss the nursery daily activities with the children.

To learn about the sequencing of activities.

Materials and preparation

Card for the symbols or pictures and Velcro or Blu-tack to attach the card so that the sequence can be displayed. Drawing and writing materials and relevant pictures or symbols.

What to do

1. Decide which are the main activities for the home and nursery that happen every day.

2. Choose from the following examples or add ones relevant to the children's nursery day:

   Wake up

   Jump out of bed

   Have breakfast

   Go to nursery

   Meet my friends and my teacher

   Play

   Drink some water or milk

   Enjoy a story

   Sing some songs

   Go home.

3. For each example and with the children, make a card using a symbol or a picture that depicts the activity. Discuss with the children why it is an appropriate picture to choose.

4. Discuss with the children the sequence for the cards introducing appropriate relevant vocabulary which reminds them of the activity, such as the names of the stories and songs that they have enjoyed. Take the children to the different parts of the nursery where these activities take place so that the children associate the activity with its location.

5. When the discussion has finished, assemble the cards in the correct sequence and display more permanently so that the sequence can be clearly seen by the children and can be used by them to know what it is that they can do at nursery. Refer frequently to the sequence and help the children to use the vocabulary and to say how they will plan their activities.

Extension activities

1. Ask the children to arrange the sequence by themselves, if possible naming the activities as the cards are placed.

2. The children can draw their own sequence of activities using their own picture ideas. Discuss with the children what they have drawn and repeat the names of the nursery activities with them.

3. Support the children to use and extend the phrases that accompany the pictures, for example 'I have toast for my breakfast' or 'I like singing "The wheels on the bus"'.

Key vocabulary
Morning, afternoon, lunch time, home time. All the vocabulary associated with the daily nursery activities.

Links with Early Years Foundation Stage curriculum for personal, social and emotional development
Show increasing confidence in new situations. Seek and delight in new experiences. Show increasing independence in selecting and carrying out activities. Have a sense of personal identity. Feel safe and secure and demonstrate a sense of trust. Make connections between different parts of their life experience.

My home

 ### Activity name: My home

Objectives

To introduce vocabulary connected with the home.

To learn the names of some shapes.

To practise counting up to 5.

Materials and preparation
Ideally this activity would take place with small-world activity play items using the house and the furniture. If this is not available the activity can still be carried out by drawing a very simple outline of a house which is divided into four rooms: kitchen, sitting room or lounge, bedroom and bathroom. Make sure there is a door and some windows, and perhaps a roof and chimney. Use pictures of simple furniture cut out from magazines. Initially, do not have more than five items for each room.

What to do

1. Sit round the house with the children and discuss with them the names of the rooms and the outside features such as the roof, windows and doors.

2. Look at the pictures or the house and discuss with the children the activities that take place in each room of the house that are associated with the pictures or the furniture in each room. Discuss one room at a time and remember to name each item ■ providing a context for its use.

3. Place all the pictures or small-world items on the floor and ask the children to collect all the objects associated with one room in the house. Name all the objects as they are collected and placed in the correct room.

4. Choose one child to decide which room will be named first and another child to collect up and name the appropriate items. All the children count the items as they are placed in the room.

5. The children are quite likely to mention some additional items that their home has and these could be drawn or a picture obtained and then added to the appropriate room.

Extension activities

1. Introduce the names of the shapes such as square or rectangle for the windows or door.

2. Increase the range of items to be named and placed in the appropriate room of the house.

3. Role play activities in the home corner.

Key vocabulary
Kitchen, lounge or sitting room, bathroom, bedroom, stairs, upstairs, downstairs, table, chair, television, oven, fridge, freezer, sink, bath, shower, hand basin, bed, wardrobe, books, toys, nursery bag, roof, chimney, windows and doors.

Links with Early Years Foundation Stage curriculum for personal, social and emotional development
Have a sense of personal identity. Show a strong sense of self as a member of different communities, such as their family or setting. Make connections between parts of their life experience.

See what I can do!

 ### Activity name: See what I can do !

Objectives

To develop a positive self-image in children as they celebrate what they can do.

To enable children to connect vocabulary with the appropriate action.

Materials and preparation
A large open space is needed, preferably outdoors. Check that the children have suitable footwear that enables them to move safely.

What to do

1. Begin by establishing appropriate safety rules such as the signal to be used for the children to stop and the way in which the children need to move safely by watching out for other children and not bumping into anybody.

2. Have a few short practices involving the children walking and then stopping at the chosen signal. When they are safe in doing this, move on to other activities.

3. Using the same phrase on each occasion ask the children to see if they can move according to the chosen activity. 'Can you run slowly/quickly?' Choose from the following suggestions such as: hop, skip, jump, sit down, stand up, balance on your left leg, balance on your right leg, curl up small, stretch up high, be as wide as you can, be as thin as you can.

4. Start by choosing a small number of activities and then repeating these so that the children clearly hear the instruction and can carry it out, possibly by copying the other children. On some occasions the children can measure their jumps using non-standard measures or time themselves using egg timers or digital timers.

5. When the children are confident in understanding what they have to do, personalise the activity by saying the child's name: 'Sophie, can you stretch up high?'. Encourage the reply, 'Yes, I can stretch up high' followed by the chosen activity. After a short while indicate that everyone should now join in the activity before moving on to the next child and the next activity.

6. Use another set of activities for indoors such as: sleep, wake up, laugh, smile, shout, whisper, cry, frown.

Extension activities

1. Use the traditional rhyme 'See the little bunnies sleeping' and adapt the actions and the names of the animals. The game begins with the children 'sleeping' on the floor until the part of the rhyme, 'Wake up, bunnies' when they jump up and quickly move around with bunny hops or other chosen action while the rhyme continues until it is time to stop.

    See the little bunnies sleeping

    Till it's nearly noon

    Shall we try and wake them gently

    With a merry tune?

    Oh how still … are they ill?

    Shhhhhhhhhh …

    Wake, little bunnies hop, hop, hop.

Wake, little bunnies hop, hop, hop.

Wake, little bunnies hop, hop, hop

And stop!

2. Adaptations include; 'See the little froggies sleeping' – with the froggies jumping when they wake up.

Key vocabulary
All of the action vocabulary, slowly, quickly, very fast, stop, go, ready, steady, go. The names of the animals.

Links with Early Years Foundation Stage curriculum for personal, social and emotional development
Have a positive approach to activities and events. Display high levels of involvement in activities. Demonotrates a sense of pride in own achievement. Have a positive self-image and show they are comfortable with themselves.

Feelings

 ## Activity name: Feelings

Objectives

To enable children to express how they are feeling.

To offer children some strategies for dealing with their feelings.

Materials and preparation
All Kinds of Feelings by Emma Brownjohn (Tango 1-85707-596-X). *If you're happy and you know it!* by Jan Ormerod (Oxford University Press. 0-19-272551-3). Thin card. Large sheets of paper. Writing and drawing materials.

What to do

1. Introduce the topic by reading a book such as *All Kinds of Feelings*. Encourage the children to look carefully at the illustrations so that they have the chance to recognise their own feelings. The children who are learning English as an additional language will benefit from the support of an interpreter or bilingual member of staff as this activity can be a personal and sensitive topic for some children.

2. Children need to know that it is normal and acceptable to feel sad and angry at times, and these negative emotions can be sensitively explored if the children are ready and have appropriate language support. Use examples that are relevant to the children so that they can understand the different emotions being discussed.

3. With the children, prepare two large sheets of paper that have either a large happy face or a large sad face with an appropriate title, 'I feel happy when … ' or 'I feel sad when …' Use other headings as appropriate.

4. Ask the children to draw a situation when they felt a particular type of emotion, such as feeling happy, sad, angry, excited, bored, frightened. When the drawing is finished take some time to talk with each child on an individual basis about what they have drawn, by commenting appropriately on their picture. Listen carefully to the children's comments and help them with an understanding of the emotions they have described.

5. The children can then attach their picture to the appropriate chart. Continue to comment on their drawing.

6. When all the children have stuck their pictures onto the paper discuss with them all the situations that have been drawn and, if possible, some ways of resolving situations that are worrying them. It may be helpful to discuss with the children that playing with sand and water can be very soothing activities for times when they are feeling angry or annoyed.

Extension activities

1. Introduce the book *If you're happy and you know it!* by Jan Ormerod and with the children look at the animals and the actions that they perform in order to 'do their own thing'.

2. Sing the well-known song, 'If you're happy and you know it clap your hands' with all the verses and the accompanying actions. Remember that the children will be able to join in with the actions before knowing the words of the song.

Key vocabulary

All the vocabulary connected with feelings and emotions. The vocabulary in the song, 'If you're happy and you know it clap your hands' including nod your head, stamp your feet. The names of the animals in Jan Ormerod's book.

Links with Early Years Foundation Stage curriculum for personal, social and emotional development

Show confidence in linking up with others for support and guidance. Express needs and feelings in appropriate ways. Form friendships with other children. Respond to the feelings and wishes of others.

People who help us

 ## Activity name: People who help us

Objectives

To help children understand that there are people who can help them.

To enable children to know that it is acceptable to ask for help.

To extend vocabulary connected with colour.

Materials and preparation

Books to introduce the topic such as *Does a kangaroo have a mother too?* by Eric Carle and published by Collins. A range of situation books introducing people who help us, such as the nurse, doctor, teacher, police officer. Large sheets of paper and a variety of collage material.

What to do

1. Begin with a discussion about the people who are closest to the children, who help them, and discuss the many ways in which the members of their family help them. Encourage the children to give examples of the help that they receive but also the help that they are able to give to members of their family.

2. Extend the discussion by talking about people in the community who are there to help, such as the nurse, doctor, police officer, librarian, optician, dentist and teacher.

3. Choose two occupations that will form the basis of each collage, such as nurse and police officer.

4. Ask two of the children to lie on the floor and then draw round them to have two body shapes, one for the nurse and one for the police officer.

5. With the children, sketch out the uniform and body parts, talking about what is being drawn such as the hands and feet and head and the parts of the uniform such as buttons, belt, and badges. Link with the activity called 'All about me' and the song 'Head, shoulders, knees and toes'.

6. Using a variety of collage material complete the nurse and the police officer, talking about the colour of material used and using positional language as the pieces are placed.

7. When the collages are completed, find a place for them in the nursery and then discuss with the children the ways in which they might be helped by the nurse and the police officer. Use the same structures such as 'A nurse helps us by …'. The police officer helps us by …'.

8. Write down some of the children's comments using the same sentence structure and display them with the collage. Refer frequently to the children's comments when continuing the discussion.

Extension activities

1. Extend the activity to include other people who help us.

2. Include the equipment that is used by the people who help us, such as the eye chart used by the optician or bandages used by the nurse. The children may be able to name some of the letters on the eye chart or bandage a finger as part of role play.

3. Set up the imaginative play area equipping it so that the children can use it for role play. Link it with the occupational roles chosen for further discussion.

Key vocabulary

The vocabulary connected with the occupation and the equipment used by people who help us. The names of the buildings where they work such as school, hospital, library, police station. The colours seen in the collage material. Parts of the uniform that the children are likely to be familiar with such as dress, trousers, buttons, belt, hat.

Links with Early Years Foundation Stage curriculum for personal, social and emotional development

Seek and delight in new experiences. Show confidence in linking up with others for guidance and support. Display high levels of involvement in activities. Feel safe and secure and show a sense of trust.

Keeping safe

Activity name: Keeping safe

Objectives

To help children understand the importance of keeping safe.

To help children keep safe on their way to nursery.

To find out about road safety.

Materials and preparation

Link this activity with 'People who help us' and use the resources made in that activity if they are appropriate. The police officer would link in well. This activity could be used for situations where children need to be safe such as 'Keeping safe in nursery' as an introduction to any setting's 'Golden Rules', or perhaps in a different situation such 'Keeping safe at the beach'. In this activity the focus will be on 'Keeping safe on the way to nursery'. The focus for this activity is to create a poster or display that will remind all the children about some safety rules. This learning will be backed up with the children using floor road mats, cars, lorries and other small-world play to emphasise the safety points made and also going outside using bikes, trikes and cars to create 'traffic situations'.

What to do

1. Introduce the topic by discussing with the children who brings them to nursery school, such as mummy, daddy, a grandparent or other carer, perhaps a childminder. The children are likely to be able to suggest some 'rules' that they are asked to follow in order to keep safe. Use the children's ideas and build on these. Be certain to discuss any particular hazards that are relevant to the children's own nursery.

2. During the discussion record the children's suggestions, which should be kept for future use. This can be done with drawing simple stick men pictures, highlighting part of a commercially produced road safety poster with small sticky notes put on by the children or using small-world play to act out the suggestion by the child making it.

3. As each point is discussed try to draw out from the children the reasons why a particular action is safe or unsafe. If it is thought to be unsafe offer a better solution together with the reason and then act out this situation with the children using the small-world play and the road mat.

4. Take the children outside and role play the safe crossing of a road with some children using the nursery bikes and cars, other children being pedestrians and one child using the lollipop sign. Make sure that all the children are familiar with the words 'Stop' and 'Go' using red and green colours appropriately. This activity will require some additional staffing to organise it well.

5. After the discussion and the activity ask the children to draw a picture of them coming to the nursery, if possible depicting one of the 'safety rules'. These might include:

   (a) walking near the kerb holding the hand of their parent or carer

   (b) be very careful where there are parked cars

   (c) stop before crossing a road or a path

   (d) look all round for cars, buses and bikes

   (e) listen for any traffic

   (f) walk across the road and do not run

   (g) use a zebra crossing or a place where there is a lollipop man or lollipop lady to help

   (h) if using traffic lights wait until the 'green man' indicates that it is safe to cross.

6. Display the pictures with a suitable heading and use as the basis for frequent discussion.

Extension activities

1. As the discussion takes place record the method of transport that the children use to travel to nursery which may include walking, travelling by car, travelling by taxi or perhaps on the back of a bike. Create an appropriate symbol. The children can use the computer to create a simple bar chart. Using the bar chart ask the children to place their symbol in the correct place on the graph.

2. Use the graph for discussion to introduce mathematical language such as 'more than, less than, fewer than, in total'. With the children count how many

children use each form of transport to come to nursery. Help the children to understand that the last number spoken tells them the total number of any counting and addition activity.

Key vocabulary

Police officer, lollipop man and lollipop lady, zebra crossing, traffic lights, green man, road, kerb, red, stop, go, car, bus, bike, taxi together with the chosen mathematical language.

Links with Early Years Foundation Stage curriculum for personal, social and emotional development

Show increasing confidence in linking up with others for support and guidance. Show care and concern for self. Have a sense of personal identity, have a sense of self as a member of different communities. Feel safe and secure and demonstrate a sense of trust. Demonstrate flexibility and adapt behaviour to different events, social situations and changes in routine. Value and contribute to own well-being and self-control. Make connections between different parts of their life experiences.

Summary: key principles for promoting personal, social and emotional development

■ Plan the environment so that children can be responsible for and participate in daily, routine nursery activities.

■ Promote self-esteem and independence in as many ways as possible.

■ Remember to give encouragement and praise for the effort made by children.

■ Build connections between the children's home culture and language and their nursery experiences.

CHAPTER 7

Practical activities for communication, language and literacy

This chapter considers ways in which practitioners can introduce a broad range of activities which enable children to build their communication skills, enjoy language experiences and develop emerging literacy skills. Building confidence and developing skills in communication are an important aspect of daily nursery activities for all children. However, for children learning English as an additional language this is a high priority as the means by which the children can take part in shared nursery experiences, express their needs and feelings, and begin to build relationships with their peers and with staff. Early years practitioners are generally skilled in promoting language development within the context of play and other shared learning experiences, and bilingual children need these contexts in order to build their language skills and gain confidence in communicating. First and additional languages can both be developed and supported within the context of imaginative and role play. Staff who are able to tune in to children and to build a comprehensive understanding of the children and the different ways in which they communicate will be able to develop language through activities that are of interest and have relevance to them.

The Early Years Foundation Stage planning promotes all aspects of communication including listening and speaking, together with reading and writing. Listening is a very important aspect of learning any language, and practitioners need to ensure that the children are listening carefully before beginning any activity. In settings where emergent literacy skills are planned to be part of all nursery activities young bilingual children will be able to gain additional language skills in a manner similar to the ways in which they learnt their first language. They need a rich experience of conversations, stories told and read, and songs and poems, all set within a framework of warm relationships. The children will recognise the language of books and gradually begin to introduce this language into their own speech. One child, while playing a small-world game, remarked that the farmer would be going away for a 'year and a day'. As part of their play the children will be able to draw, paint, use computers and engage in other mark-making activities. They will be able to enjoy activities which offer a gentle introduction to reading by recognising print and other visual images in their environment.

All the children in the reception class had been enjoying the *Spot* books. Their teacher knew that they enjoyed looking at the adventures of Spot and introduced the children to other stories which had dogs as their main characters. They particularly liked hearing about the adventures of Biff and Buff and their owner, Mr Pockets, all of whom had their adventures retold in the book *The Pocket Dogs* by Margaret Wild, published by Scholastic Press. Kenta spent a long time looking at the text and the illustrations and then

(Continued)

went to the creative workshop area to paint a picture of Biff and Buff. He took the painting to the nursery nurse working in his classroom and gave her the picture saying 'dog'. She commented enthusiastically about his picture and asked him if he wanted to write anything about his picture. Kenta said 'dog' and he copied what the nursery nurse had written. She told Kenta's mother of his achievements when he was collected from school. Several days later Kenta's mother was delighted as she told the nursery nurse that at the weekend she had taken Kenta to the swimming pool and while he was playing in the learner pool he had looked at a notice informing swimmers about the water depth. Kenta had pointed to the word 'depth' and said, 'That's d for dog'. Kenta had been able to take his learning about print and recognise a letter that interested him in a different context and environment.

Young children need the opportunity to recognise their own community languages as well as English, and to become visually literate. Practical suggestions for activities which promote the development of communication, language and literacy skills follow.

- Days of the week
- Months
- Weather
- Seasons
- My favourite story character
- My favourite story
- Action rhymes
- Traditional nursery tales.

Days of the week

Activity name: Days of the week

Objectives

To introduce the vocabulary for days of the week and the names of some fruit.

To use the days of the week in the context of a story or an activity.

To encourage children to listen attentively.

To practise counting using numbers up to 10.

Materials and preparation

Simple flash cards depicting the names of the days of the week. *Where does Thursday go?* by Janeen Brian, published by Southwood Books. *The Very Hungry Caterpillar* by Eric Carle. A large dice and some drawings or pictures of a selection of the foods eaten by the hungry caterpillar. Six drawings of each of the foods chosen from the story *The Very Hungry Caterpillar*.

What to do

1. As part of the start of each day or each nursery session begin the welcome group activity by introducing the day of the week, the month and the date. This can be done by the use of a simple chart which is completed by the children taking it in turns to collect the correct labels for the day, month and date. By doing this on a daily basis the children will soon recognise the initial sounds in the names of the week and recognise the letters which represent the sounds and the numbers making up the date. Remember to have some fun activities such as 'Find the day that comes after Thursday' and 'Find the day that comes before Friday'.

2. When the children are familiar with the names of the days of the week and can recognise the words on the cards, make up a sequencing game so that the children can arrange the letters in the correct sequence. On a different occasion begin the sequence with a different day of the week.

3. Introduce the story of *The Very Hungry Caterpillar* and enjoy the story and the illustrations with the children.

4. Spend some time discussing with the children the food that the caterpillar ate on each day of the week. Discuss with the children which their favourite/least favourite day would be if they were able to share the food eaten by the Hungry Caterpillar on a particular day.

5. With the children draw on thin card some pictures of the foods eaten by the caterpillar, which include: apples, pears, plums, strawberries, oranges, chocolate cake, ice cream, pickle, cheese, salami, lollipop, cherry pie, sausage, cupcake, watermelon. A drawing of the Very Hungry Caterpillar is also needed and is placed inside a hoop.

6. As the children listen to the story and the days of the week are mentioned together with the food to be eaten, the children take it in turns to jump up, collect the appropriate food and place it in the hoop with the caterpillar.

7. 'Jumping Jack' is another active game to play which encourages listening skills. The children sit in a space and are reminded to listen very carefully. Staff choose which fruit they will name and which activity, such as 'Jump up if you like eating apples' or 'Clap twice if you like eating pears' or 'Hop round in a circle if you like eating chocolate cake'.

Extension activities

1. This activity can be extended by using the story of *The Very Hungry Caterpillar* and linking it with learning and using numbers 1–6. Choose six of the foods in the story and have ready six cards of each of the foods.

2. The children take it in turns to throw the die and to call out the number that appears on the dice. They then collect the number of cards according to the number on the dice and the food that they have chosen. Encourage the children to call out the number on the dice and to count out the 'food cards' as they are collected. 'I've got 1, 2, 3, 4 apples' or 'I've got 1, 2, 3, 4, 5 lollipops'. There will be some spare cards at the end of the game for all the children to count out together to see what is left.

3. Sometimes when the game is finished the children could be helped to make a bar chart graph to record which foods each of them collected in the game.

4. Another extension activity would be to enjoy the story *Where does Thursday go?* when Splodge and his friend Humbug endeavour to solve the puzzle of where does Thursday go before Friday comes?

Key vocabulary
Days of the week. The foods enjoyed by the Very Hungry Caterpillar. Numbers 1–6.

Links with the Early Years Foundation Stage for communication, language and literacy
Listen to stories with increasing attention and recall. Join in with repeated refrains, anticipating key events and important phrases. Listen to stories with increasing attention and recall. Use vocabulary focused on objects and people who are of increasing importance to them. Distinguish one sound from another.

Months

 ## Activity name: When's my birthday?

Objectives

To introduce the months of the year through finding out about birthdays.

To talk with other children and staff to find out when everyone celebrates their birthday.

To learn the names of some colours.

To know and use numbers from 1–12.

Materials and preparation
Thin card. Paints. Sponges and other print-making tools.

What to do

1. Introduce the months of the year in the welcome group at the beginning of the session in a similar manner to the way in which the days of the week were introduced.

2. With the children, make a large train followed by 12 passenger carriages. The children may be interested to draw one of the famous bullet trains from Japan called the 'Shinkansen'. This would be particularly relevant if there were Japanese children in the group. The train and the passenger carriages can be painted using sponge painting and as many different types of painting and printing as possible, including potato printing, splatter painting and marble painting. Use different colours for the passenger carriages. Remember to talk with the children about what is happening and the colours and 'tools' used.

3. Discuss with the children what name to choose for the train and name each of the passenger carriages with the name of one of the months. Help the children to write these names on the train and passenger carriages, discussing them with the children as the names are written.

4. When the train is finished, assist the children to find out among themselves when their own birthdays are before talking with the other children in the group and the staff to find out about their birthdays. Write the children's names and stick them onto the correct carriage. Another way of recording the birthdays is to ask the children to draw something which is very special to them and which they will recognise as theirs and then add their name before fixing the drawing and their name to the appropriate month.

5. Display the train and passenger carriages in the nursery and refer to it especially at the start of each month or when a particular birthday is celebrated.

6. Help the children to say the names of the months in the correct sequence and to take part in the game 'What comes before and what comes after a particular month?'.

Extension activities

1. Have ready some cards with the names of the months written on them and number each month from 1 to 12. Use different shapes and colours for the cards, such as square, green January, and round, yellow February. Use appropriate pictures or symbols to help the children recognise the month.

2. When the children can recognise the name of each month and the shape and the colour, extend the activity into a number activity. Take it in turns for a child to call out or to point to a number from 1 to 12. Another child picks out the card with the correct number and accompanying month.

Key vocabulary
The months of the year. Numbers 1–12.

Links with the Early Years Foundation Stage for communication, language and literacy
Respond to simple instructions. Use action, sometimes with limited talk, that is largely concerned with the 'here and now'. Understand the concept of a word. Build up vocabulary that reflects their breadth of experiences.

Weather

 ## Activity name: What's the weather like today?

Objectives

To introduce the vocabulary connected with different weather conditions.

To use phrases describing the weather.

To introduce traditional weather rhymes and a weather game.

Materials and preparation

Materials to make a simple chart to use at the 'welcome group' time to depict the day of the week, month, date and the weather. Cards for the chart which describe the weather. A collection of clothes which are relevant to particular types of weather. Large shapes such as triangle, square and circle.

What to do

1. Have a discussion with the group of children about the current weather conditions. Use the weather that the children are experiencing on that day to begin the discussion. Use simple vocabulary such as 'It's sunny today' or 'Today it's raining'.

2. Expand the discussion to include the different seasons of the year with the most familiar weather situations of each season included, such as snow in winter and windy weather in autumn.

3. After the discussion decide with the children which weather words will be included for each season.

4. With the children, make flash cards which will fit onto the chart and have simple weather statements on them such as 'It's windy today' or 'It's chilly today'. Keep to the same structure so that the children will recognise the sentences and be able to repeat them.

5. Encourage the children to add a relevant symbol to each of the flash cards. They could draw a small picture or cut one from a magazine.

6. When using the chart during the welcome session, discuss the type of weather with the children and then encourage the children to take it in turns to choose the appropriate card to place on the chart repeating the weather phrase when they are confident.

7. Use the following question as part of the welcome session, 'What's the weather like today?' The children can then reply appropriately to this question.

Extension activities

1. Gather together a range of clothes, hats, shoes and other garments that are related to particular types of weather such as sunny weather, wet weather and snow.

2. With the children make large shapes such as triangles, squares and circles. Decorate the shapes as creatively as possible, with finger painting, sponge painting or weather collages.

3. With the children, decide which shape will represent which weather, such as the sunny circle, the wet triangle and the snowy square. Discuss with the children which colours are most closely linked with each type of weather and use these colours for the decoration. A suitable picture could be attached to the shape to help the children remember which shape is connected with which type of weather.

4. Using the collection of clothing, discuss with the children which item of clothing is linked with each type of weather and encourage the children to take it in turns to place the item onto the correct shape.

5. Model an appropriate response from the children, such as 'I'm putting the woolly hat into the snowy square' or 'I'm putting the sun hat into the sunny circle'.

6. Before the game starts remember to make sure that the children know the names for the items of clothing and their link to each type of weather.

7. If possible link some relevant weather rhymes such as:

    The sun has got his hat on

    Hip, hip, hip hooray.

    The sun has got his hat on

    And is coming out today.

    or

    Rain, rain, go away

    Come again another day.

Key vocabulary
Weather words such as sunny, warm, hot, cold, chilly, rain, wet, thunder, lightning, windy, snow, hail, rainbow. Clothes words such as, hat, sun hat, woolly hat, bobble hat, coat, raincoat, anorak, sweater, jumper, trousers, skirt, dress, gloves, mittens, scarf, swimming costume, wellington boots, sandals, shoes, socks tights.

Links with the Early Years Foundation Stage for communication, language and literacy
Use simple statements and questions often linked to gestures. Use simple grammatical structures. Respond to simple instructions. Use vocabulary focused on objects and

people who are of particular importance to them. Build up vocabulary that reflects their breadth of experiences.

Seasons

 ## Activity name: 'Spring, summer, autumn and winter'

Objectives

To introduce the different seasons of the year.

To link the months of the year with the seasons.

To link a particular season with seasonal activities.

To practise counting forwards and backwards.

To introduce mathematical language.

Materials and preparation

A large paper plate for each child. Paper fastener. Card for the snowmen. Pictures showing each of the seasons.

What to do

1. Introduce the names of the seasons; spring, summer, autumn and winter.

2. Help the children to understand the meanings of the words by looking at the pictures and discussing the various signs connected with each season.

3. Divide the paper plate into four quarters and use each section for one of the seasons. Remember to use vocabulary such as circle, quarters and numbers 1 to 4.

4. Help the children to draw, paint or cut out symbols or pictures connected with each of the seasons and glue the pictures onto the appropriate section of the paper plate.

5. Fix a large pointer with an arrow into the centre of the paper plate. The pointer needs to be able to swivel easily round the paper plate.

6. Discuss with the children which months might be associated with each season.

   Spring: March, April and May.

   Summer: June, July and August.

   Autumn: September, October and November.

   Winter: December, January and February.

7. With the children make a chart which shows which months fall into each season. Use pictures or symbols to help the children recognise each of the seasons.

8. The children take it in turns to call out a month and all the children turn the pointer on their season plate to the right season and then name the season. Remember to praise good effort.

Extension activities

1. This activity links with the winter season but can be adapted for the other seasons.

2. Each child needs to make a symbol connected with winter, such as a snowman.

3. Cut out large, simple snowman shapes and decorate with a woolly hat or scarf. Have different colours for the hats and scarves so that these colours can be named as they are being used.

4. Place a number on each of the snowmen, counting out the numbers with the children as they are being put onto the snowmen.

5. Each child holds a snowman and is asked to 'line up' in ascending order.

6. As their number is called out in ascending order they jump forward to make a new line.

7. The children take it in turns to be the one to call out the numbers.

8. The game can be repeated with the children 'lining up' in descending order.

9. Change the numbered snowmen that the children hold so that they have a range of experiences in sorting themselves out by holding different numbers.

Key vocabulary
The seasons and the months of the year. Numbers. Circle, quarter, snowman, woolly hat, scarf.

Links with the Early Years Foundation Stage for communication, language and literacy
Respond to simple instructions. Talk activities through, reflecting on and modifying what they are doing. Build up vocabulary that reflects the breadth of their experiences.

My favourite story character

 ## Activity name: The witch in *Room on the Broom*

Objectives

To encourage children to enjoy stories.

To encourage creativity and imagination.

To show awareness of rhymes and enjoy rhyming activities.

Materials and preparation

Several copies of the chosen book, a taped recording of the story, a Big Book copy. Dual-language text of the chosen story, if available. Creative materials.

What to do

1. The children will have many suggestions for their favourite story characters. One of their favourite characters may well be the witch with the long ginger plait in the story *Room on the Broom* by Julia Donaldson, published by Macmillan Children's Books. The activities suggested here will be based on that book but can be adapted to suit the children's favourite character in a different storybook.

2. Introduce the story to the children by first looking at the cover pictures and introducing the witch and her wand, the broomstick, the cauldron and the cat, the moon and the stars. The children can take it in turns to point to the main items on the front cover as they are discussed.

3. Discuss with the children the possibility of adventures on a broomstick and what they think might happen in the story. Presenting the story in an interesting way encourages the children to want more of the story and to be ready to listen carefully. If this is the first time the children have heard the story then, without spoiling it, make sure that the children understand the key vocabulary and the main storyline. Have the story available on tape so that the children can hear it at any time. Make sure that all the children have access to the dual-language text if available.

4. Using the Big Book if possible, share the story with the children, making sure they can see the pictures. Add suspense and take on the voices of the different characters, especially those of the witch and the fierce dragon. Involve the children in the story and make sure that there is sufficient time for them to look at the pictures.

5. When the story is finished discuss with the children some of the witch's adventures. Choose one or two adventures and be guided by the children as to the choice. One way of them choosing the adventure to be discussed is to give a child the book and let them turn to their favourite picture.

6. Encourage the children to describe the witch by looking carefully at the pictures and using the vocabulary and the phrases, or part of the phrases, contained in the story, such as 'a very tall hat', 'long ginger hair which she wore in a plait', 'away blew the bow from her long ginger plait', 'they searched for the wand but no wand could be found'.

7. Draw round the outline of one of the children and then assist the children to add the witch's very tall hat, long ginger plait with bow and her wand. Use different creative techniques to complete the picture of the witch, remembering to use the key vocabulary in as many ways as possible.

8. Using different techniques such as sponge painting, printing, straw painting or marble painting, create a backing paper for the display depicting some of the pictures from the story, such as the stars and the moon or the dragon and the 'horrible beast' with 'four frightful heads'.

9. Include in the display some speech bubbles with the comments of the children, together with some key vocabulary and phrase from the story. Use some of the rhymes from the story and draw the attention of the children to some of the rhymes and the enjoyable sounds created.

10. The other characters from the story can be included in similar activities. The children will enjoy creating displays which include the cat, the dog, the bird, the frog, together with the dragon and the horrible beast.

Extension activities

1. Discuss with the children the part of the story where the 'BROOM SNAPPED IN TWO' followed by the filling of the cauldron to create a 'TRULY MAGNIFICENT BROOM'. Show the children how these phrases are written in capital letters in the story.

2. Gather together some suitable props and role-play the scene of the frog, cat, bird and dog helping the witch to magic up a new broomstick.

3. Discuss with the children what their spell will be and what items they will choose to put into the cauldron.

4. Encourage the children to take it in turns to be the witch who conjures up the spell.

5. After the role play discuss with the children what their new broomstick will be like.

6. Look carefully at the illustration by Axel Scheffler and encourage the children to use their imagination to think of special luxuries for the witch, cat, dog, bird and frog.

7. Ask the children to create their own new broomstick and to draw and paint their new creation. Make a display of these new inventions and add the children's comments about their own broomstick.

Key vocabulary
The main vocabulary from the story based on the characters and the objects seen in the illustrations, including squirrel, owl, sheep, fish, lily, cone, twig and bone.

Links with the Early Years Foundation Stage for communication, language and literacy
Listen to stories with increasing attention or recall. Join in with repeated refrains, anticipating key events and important phrases. Have some favourite stories, rhymes, songs,

poems or jingles. Enjoy rhyming and rhythmic activities. Show interest in illustrations and print in books and print in the environment. Have favourite books. Begin to be aware of the way stories are structured.

My favourite story

 ## Activity name: *Tales from Acorn Wood – Postman Bear*

Objectives

To encourage children to enjoy stories.

To encourage participation in storytelling.

To make links with everyday events in stories and in children's own lives.

Materials and preparation

Several copies of the chosen book. A Big Book if available. A recording of the story. Dual-language texts of the chosen book, if possible. Creative materials. Objects included in the book such as letters and party invitations. Cooking equipment and ingredients.

What to do

1. The children will have their own suggestion for their favourite book. On this occasion the activities will be centred round the story of Postman Bear, published by Macmillan Children's Books, written by Julia Donaldson and illustrated by Axel Scheffler .

2. Introduce the story by looking with the children at the front cover of the book. Discuss with the children the letters or birthday cards that they enjoy getting in the post. Talk about the postman or postwoman who comes to their house and the uniform that is worn. The story has quite a simple outline so that it should easily be followed by the children. Ensure that they understand the vocabulary connected with the birthday party and encourage them to join in the counting. Make sure that all the children have access to the dual-language text and the taped story.

3. Using the Big Book if possible, share the story with the children and make sure that they can see the pictures. Enable the children to take it in turns to lift the flaps to see the squirrel eating the acorn, the mole who lives in his hole and to peep in the oven to see what is cooking! Encourage the children to join in the counting of the letters, 1, 2 and 3.

4. When the story is finished, talk about the animals such as mole, squirrel and frog that appear in the story and the part they play in Bear's birthday party.

5. Discuss with the children the preparations that are made for a birthday party and link these ideas with the way that Bear prepares by making a cake and sending out party invitations.

6. Help each of the children to make an invitation to a small celebration that will be shared with all the children in the group. Encourage all the children to write their own name or use mark-making to represent their name on the invitation and to address it to one of the children in the class. Make sure that the addressing of the invitations is organised so that all the children in the class receive one. Do not forget the staff! Pop all the addressed invitations into the postbox!

7. At a suitable time, open the postbox and take out the addressed invitations which are delivered by the children to each other. Encourage the children to read the names out before delivering them. They may need some assistance at this point from the other children or the staff.

8. Decide on the preparations for the celebration and involve the children. It can be a simple celebration with drinks and sandwiches prepared and laid out by the children. If cooking facilities are available, a cake made out of healthy ingredients could be prepared by the children.

9. At the celebration play 'Pass the parcel'. Look at the parcels that are brought to Bear's birthday party by mole, squirrel and frog.

10. Put the children's names into the parcel to be found each time the parcel is unwrapped. As the names are found ask the children to help decide what activity is to be carried out such as 'jump five times'.

Extension activities

1. After enjoying the story again, draw the children's attention to the rhymes that are included in the story such as:

    Bear is writing letters.

    One, two, three.

    Bear goes out to post them.

    Who lives in this tree?

Ask the children to decide which words rhyme.

2. Children can gain great enjoyment from making up very simple rhymes using animals as a starting point. One child who was almost 3 years old enjoyed the story of Postman Bear and made up a rhyme followed quickly by other children joining in the activity:

    Have you seen a mole living in a hole?

    Have you seen a pig sitting on a twig?

Have you seen a lamb eating bread and jam?

Have you seen a hen writing with a pen?

Have you seen a bear sitting on a chair?

I can see one over there!

3. Encourage the children to make up their own rhymes. Do not be surprised if there are some nonsense rhymes as well!

4. Some of the children may be able to make up similar rhymes in their first language.

Key vocabulary
The key vocabulary from the story including the names of the animals and the objects seen in the story, including acorn, letter, party invitation, canoe, spade, rake, kitchen, oven, door. It is also helpful for the children to know the phrases from the story of Postman Bear, 'Happy Birthday, Bear!' and 'Come to my party'.

Links with the Early Years Foundation Stage for communication, language and literacy
Listen to stories with increasing attention and recall. Use vocabulary focused on objects and people who are of particular importance to them. Enjoy rhyming and rhythmic activities. Listen to others in one-to-one or small groups when conversation interests them. Handle books carefully. Sometimes give meaning to marks as they draw and point.

Action rhymes

 ## Activity name: Counting rhymes

Objectives

To participate in rhymes through actions and gestures.

To practise counting.

To enjoy rhymes.

To introduce simple language to compare size.

Materials and preparation
A collection of traditional action rhymes such as *This Little Puffin* compiled by Elizabeth Matterson and published by Puffin Books, or the collection of rhymes by Opal Dunn, *Hippety-hop, Hippety-hay* published by Frances Lincoln Limited. Large sheets of paper. Thickish paint for the hand prints. Plenty of soap and water to clean the children's hands.

What to do

1. Decide which selection of rhymes will form the starting point for this activity. It is best to choose rhymes that have a great deal of repetition, are fairly short and have vocabulary that the children may already be familiar with. The rhymes should also have actions that the children can join in with as this will be the way in which they first participate with the rhyme. Encourage the children to join in with the last word of any rhyming line and pause for a short time to give them time to join in.

2. A possible selection of rhymes could include:

> Fingers like to wiggle, waggle
>
> Wiggle, waggle, wiggle, waggle,
>
> Fingers like to wiggle, waggle,
>
> Right in front of me.

Repeat the first three lines and change the last line each time.

verse 2 – high above my head

verse 3 – low behind my back

verse 4 – way out to my right

verse 5 – way out to my left (adapted from a rhyme in *This Little Puffin* compiled by Elizabeth Matterson).

> If you're happy and you know it clap your hands
>
> If you're happy and you know it clap your hands
>
> If you're happy and you know it and you really want to show it
>
> If you're happy and you know it clap your hands. (Traditional)

This is the way we clap with our hands

> Clap with our hands
>
> Clap with our hands
>
> This is the way we clap with our hands
>
> One, two, three. (adapted from a rhyme in *Hippety-hop, Hippety-hay* by Opal Dunn)

3. Any hand-printing activity needs to be carefully supervised and carried out with a small number of children at a time. Be very clear with the directions as to where the children should go when they have finished their hand-printing. Use this opportunity to have a range of colours for the paints and a range of shapes, colours and textures for the paper.

4. Discuss with the children the various choices that they have with regard to paint and paper. When the choices have been made help the children to carry out the handprinting perhaps deciding with them how many handprints they will make.

5. When all the children and staff have had their turn and the prints are dry, discuss with all of the children who has the largest/smallest/narrowest/widest hands. Use the actual prints for the children to measure their hands against so that they understand the language being used.

6. Create a display which shows gradation related to size. Have one display starting with the smallest hand size and another display starting with the largest hand size. Model the sentence 'This is the smallest/largest hand' and when the children are confident they can use this sentence in response to the question, 'Where is the smallest/largest hand?' with the less confident children pointing to the appropriate hand.

7. Any 'spare' handprints can be adapted for a display connected with hedgehogs.

Extension activities

1. Carry out similar activities centred round the children's feet and creating some foot prints.

2. Adapt the rhymes to refer to feet:

    'If you're happy and you know it stamp your feet'

    and

    'This is the way you stamp with your feet'

    or a marching song such as:

    > Left, right, left, right,
    >
    > Marching down the street,
    >
    > Left, right, left, right,
    >
    > Who will we meet? (from *Hippety-hop, Hippety-hay* by Opal Dunn)

3. Remember to include any first language rhymes that are linked to the chosen theme and help all the children in the class to learn these rhymes.

Key vocabulary
Fingers, hands, feet, foot, head, back, left right, wiggle, waggle, clap, stamp.

Links with the Early Years Foundation Stage for communication, language and literacy
Use simple statements and questions often linked to gestures. Respond to simple instructions. Build up vocabulary that reflects the breadth of experiences. Use intonation, rhythm and phrasing to make their meaning clear to others.

Traditional nursery tales

 Activity name: *Goldilocks and the Three Bears*

Objectives

To encourage the children to listen carefully.

To encourage the children to join in with the telling of the story.

To help children understand how a story can develop in a predictable manner.

To introduce mathematical language for comparison.

To introduce the traditional language of stories and nursery tales.

Materials and preparation

If the story is to be told rather than read make sure that sufficient preparation is carried out so that the storyteller is confident and enthusiastic when telling the story. A story that is told rather than read benefits from enabling the storyteller to build a closer rapport with the children. Use props to increase the enjoyment of the children and to help them understand the story. On this occasion the props need to be related to the story of *Goldilocks and the Three Bears Using* items from small-world play, including tables, chair and beds. On another telling of the story the props could be three teddy bears and three bowls of different sizes and a doll suitably dressed to resemble Goldilocks. Creative materials will be needed for the display.

What to do

1. Discuss with the children the way in which many stories begin and end. When they hear 'Once upon time' they will know that it is the beginning of the story and the time to listen very carefully. When they hear 'and they all lived happily ever after' they will know that the story has finished. When the children are confident about the use of these phrases, encourage the children to take it in turns to begin and end a story.

2. Tell the story of *Goldilocks and the Three Bears* keeping the structure of the story simple and using the props to involve the children and to maintain their interest. If possible encourage the children to use the props appropriately at the correct point in the story.

3. Remember to be consistent in the choice of important vocabulary and emphasise the parts of the story that in time the children will be able to join in with, such as:

'Father Bear was a big bear.'

'Mother Bear was a medium-sized bear.'

'Baby Bear was a small bear.'

'The porridge in Father Bear's big bowl was too hot.'

'The porridge in Mother Bear's medium-sized bowl was too cold.'

'The porridge in Baby Bear's small bowl was just right.'

'Father Bear's big chair was too high.'

'Mother Bear's medium-sized chair was too wide.'

'Baby Bear's small chair was just right.'

'Father Bear's big bed was too hard.'

'Mother Bear's medium-sized bed was too soft.'

'Baby Bear's small bed was just right.'

and then the relevant phrases which describe the various reactions of the bears when they find their porridge bowls, their chairs and their beds – 'Someone has been eating my porridge', 'Someone has been sitting in my chair' and 'Someone has been sleeping in my bed'. Remember to take on the various voices and characters of the bears and to finish with the amazing finding of Goldilocks in Baby Bear's bed.

4. Remember that the children may know very similar stories in their first language. If possible, help them to tell the story in their first language using the story props.

Extension activities

1. As the children become familiar with the story, make the imaginative play area into the home of the three bears. Discuss with the children which furniture and other items will be needed in the bears' home.

2. On another occasion the children could act out the tale while listening to the retelling of the story. Leave gaps in the story for the children to say the important phrases of each of the characters if they are confident enough to do so.

3. Create a display, based on the story, which clearly shows the parts of the story which relate to size, such as the bears, the bowls of porridge, the chairs and the beds. Help the children to use vocabulary such as 'bigger than' or 'smaller than'.

4. It may be possible to make some porridge for the children to taste. (As with any cooking or food-based activity, remember to inform parents and check for food allergies that any child may have. Have ready a suitable food alternative so that all the children can be included in the activity.)

Key vocabulary

Goldilocks and the names of the Three Bears, big, medium and small. Too hot, too cold, too hard, too soft, just right. House, table, chair, bed. Porridge.

Links with the Early Years Foundation Stage for communication, language and literacy

Have some favourite stories, rhymes, songs, poems or jingles. Join in with repeated refrains, anticipating key events and important phrases. Listen to stories with increasing attention and recall. Listen to others in one-to-one or-small groups when conversation interests them.

Summary: key principles for developing communication, language and literacy skills

- Remember the importance of context in developing language skills.

- Tune in to children and encourage all efforts made by the children to communicate.

- Keep in mind the ways in which young children learnt their first language.

- Use this first language approach to help children learn an additional language.

- Support the children's first language and encourage their first language contributions.

- Offer a wealth of opportunities to enjoy and share conversation, stories and rhymes.

Practical activities for problem solving, reasoning and numeracy

This chapter considers the various ways that practitioners can plan for mathematically linked activities and build on the experiences that the children have previously enjoyed in their home environment. Practitioners who are planning for mathematical experiences with in the Early Years Foundation stage need to organise activities and learning opportunities which enable the children to find out more about numbers as labels and to have the opportunity to explore number situations such as counting on and counting back. Children also benefit from experiences which relate to shape, space, measuring and recognition of pattern. Practitioners can not only help children to name shapes correctly, but also support them when they think about what makes a certain shape a square and not a triangle. When children have enjoyed a variety of mathematical experiences they need the time to talk with other children and staff in order to understand and make sense of these experiences. After these activities the next step is to enable children to make a record of their mathematical experiences and findings. Simple ways of recording can include drawing pictures, making a tally count where each mark represents one unit and a group bar chart where all members of the group add a symbol to record their individual contribution. Computers can also be used to make a tally. Many children will make marks which represent numbers and then quickly move on to using recognisable numerals to record their findings.

François aged 4½ knew how to count to 20 in French which was his first language. In his nursery school his teacher had asked his help in teaching some of the children how to count to 5 in French. They all enjoyed counting in French and very soon François was also able to count to 5 in English. He was part of a small group who were working together to make a display to accompany the rhyme '5 little ducks went swimming one day, over the pond and far away'. The children were singing part of the rhyme as they created the pond from blue splatter paint. François heard and recognised the numbers but made his first contribution by joining in 'quack, quack, quack, quack'. The next day the children used some collage materials to make the ducks, and the teacher encouraged the children to count the ducks as they said the rhyme. She showed them the number line in the room and they all counted backwards from 5 to 1. In the afternoon François asked his teacher if he could use the computer to write and print the numbers 1 to 5. Francois had gained in confidence and wanted to continue to know more about counting in English. He soon could count to 20 in English and wanted to write the numbers not only on the computer but also on the small whiteboard that was in the room.

(Continued)

(Continued)

During small-group work, bilingual staff can facilitate the children's participation in activities using their first language and then support their early acquisition of some mathematical language in English. All the children in the group can learn how to count in different languages and can sometimes use these languages for everyday counting games. The *Practice Guidance for the Early Years Foundation Stage* gives guidance to the practitioner regarding building positive relationships in relation to this area of learning: 'Support children who use a means of communication other than spoken English to develop and understand specific mathematical language while valuing knowledge of problem solving, reasoning and numeracy in the language or communication system that they use at home (DfES, 2007: 61).

It is important for all staff to enable children to take forward their own mathematical ideas and to build on these concepts in order to extend mathematical knowledge within the context of play. Skilled practitioners plan and resource play from a mathematical perspective so that the children are working towards specific learning intentions. There are several resources for mathematical activities on the excellent website of Sir Robert Hitcham's Primary School in Suffolk – www.hitchams.sch.uk. Staff who are able to play alongside the children can effectively model mathematical language and sensitively extend understanding and knowledge by building on what the children already know. They can also help the children to have a positive attitude towards mathematics, which will be of benefit in later learning. Many children will have had a wealth of mathematical experiences at home when accompanying their parent or carer to the shops, enjoying number stories and rhymes and using numbers on mobile phones, calculators, computers and other digital equipment. On any nursery day the children are likely to play with sand and water offering many experiences for measuring and then to share stories and rhymes that have a number interest. Indoor and outdoor play can have mathematical links that enable children to understand and practise mathematical skills and knowledge. The outdoor play area can be equipped with resources for mathematical experiences and ways of recording these experiences such as notebooks or small whiteboards.

Practical suggestions for activities which promote the development of problem solving, reasoning and numeracy

- Goldilocks's picnic

- 1, 2, 3 – What's in that tree?

- *Three Billy Goats Gruff*

- Busy bikes

- Dizzy dinosaurs

- Who lives in this house?

- Best foot forward!

- Flippity flop!

Counting

 Activity name: Goldilocks's picnic

Objectives

To enable children to count from 1 to 6.

To give practice in the recognition of number patterns on a dice.

To recognise shapes such as triangles, squares or circles.

To understand one-to-one correspondence.

Materials and preparation

The story of *Goldilocks and the Three Bears* to be read or told. A Big Book copy and a dual-language text copy if available. A simple board game format to lead from the house of the three bears to Goldilocks's garden. A counter for each child and a large dice.

What to do

1. Tell or read the story of the *Goldilocks and the Three Bears*. At the end of the story introduce the idea that Goldilocks's was sorry that she had eaten the porridge and had broken Baby Bear's chair. After Goldilocks's had apologised to the bears she invited them to her house to have a picnic in her garden.

2. Show the children the format for the board game and tell them how each section represents a step towards Goldilocks's house. The game can be played by a small group of children, ideally no more than four as there then can only be three bears and one Goldilocks!

3. After each child has chosen a counter and placed it at the start of the game ask the children to decide the order in which they will play the game. One way is for each child to throw the dice and the child with the highest number starts first, followed by the next highest number and so on. Take time in discussing which number is the highest and in helping the children to recognise the various patterns on the dice associated with each number. When the children have decided in which order they will take their turns in throwing the dice, it is helpful if everyone changes places so that they are sitting in the correct order as this helps children to know whose turn it is.

4. Each child throws the dice and moves along the track. Many children need help in remembering that as they move forward, the next square to the one that they have landed on is counted as one. Encourage all the children to count out loud as the counter is moved.

5. Remember to count the number of dots on the dice with the children if necessary and, over time, to encourage the children to see the pattern on the dice and to recognise the number pattern without counting and to be able to say 'That's a six'.

6. When everyone has arrived in Goldilocks's garden, discuss with the children who was first, second or third. This then introduces ordinal numbers. Ordinal numbers can also be introduced into other situations such as who is first sitting on the mat for circle time or who arrived third at nursery.

Extension activities

1. Discuss with the group of children how many plates and mugs will be needed for the picnic. They can lay out the plates and mugs on the picnic rug, making sure that there is sufficient for each person taking part in the picnic. Use positional language to describe how to place the mugs and plates on the picnic rug. On some occasions ensure that initially there are insufficient items and support the children in working out how many more plates and mugs are needed so that everyone can enjoy the picnic.

2. With the children, make some sandwiches, cutting them into triangles, squares or circles. Make certain that the sandwich fillings are appropriate for all the children, particularly those with allergies. Ensure that the children wash their hands before taking part in the activity and that they know how to use the equipment safely. Remind the children to clear up afterwards and to put all the equipment away.

3. Estimate how many sandwiches will be needed for the picnic. Count the number of sandwiches in total and then how many of each shape. Are there more circle shapes than square shapes, if so, how many?

4. Get the picnic ready and discuss with the children how the sandwiches can be shared so that everyone has an equal number and how the drink is shared so that everyone has an equal amount.

5. Enjoy the picnic and sing some counting songs such as '1, 2, 3, 4, 5, once I caught a fish alive'.

Key vocabulary
Numbers 1 to 6. Language from the story of Goldilocks. Language to play the game such as 'Move your counter'. Dice. Plate. Mug. Picnic. Sandwich. Shapes such as triangle, square and circle.

Links with the Early Years Foundation Stage curriculum for problem solving, reasoning and numeracy
Show an interest in number problems. Sometimes match number and quality correctly. Use some number language such as 'more' and 'a lot'.

Counting

 ## Activity name: 1, 2, 3 – What's in that tree?

Objectives

To give practice in counting from 1 to 10.

To use natural materials for counting.

To use mathematical language during play.

Materials and preparation

Natural items for counting such as conkers, sycamore seeds and acorns. Several containers, at least two for each child.

What to do

1. This activity could take place outside as well as inside and could be linked with seasons or other places, such as the beach, using shells. On any visit outside the nursery remember to carry out a risk assessment before the activity and to walk the route, noting places where extra care is needed. In this activity the link is with autumn with the children taking an autumnal walk to collect items such as conkers, sycamore seeds and acorns. Make sure that for the counting activity each child does not have too many items to count, usually not more than 10. Some containers are also needed to act as collecting points and later for counting. These containers could be made from natural materials or be small boxes decorated by the children to reflect the theme.

2. Get ready for the autumn walk. Encourage the children to get themselves ready and to put on their own wellington boots and coats. Discuss with the children what they might be able to see and hear. Remind the children of the safety rules for this outing and ensure that there are sufficient adults for the number of children.

3. Encourage the children to look carefully at the trees and the leaves before collecting the conkers, acorns or sycamore seeds. Help them to identify each tree and to make the links between conkers with the horse chestnut tree, acorns with the oak tree and sycamore seeds with the sycamore tree.

4. Take all the items back to the nursery and discuss what the children have seen and heard during the walk as well as what they have collected. Look carefully at the items and help the children describe what the items look and feel like, such as shiny, smooth conkers. The children should be encouraged to use both English and their first language to describe what they have collected.

5. Spread out the collection of items and sit with the children to discuss who may have more than or less than or possibly the same number of items. This is an estimating activity and should be done before counting.

6. When the children have reached their decisions then begin to count each collection of conkers, acorns or sycamore seeds. Make sure that as each child counts they move one item out of its collection box into another container so that one number relates to one item. Encourage all the children in the group to count out loud.

7. Help the children to make progress with their counting by introducing other activities such as counting up to 20, adding a certain number of items to the existing number, taking away a certain number of items and then seeing how many are left. Some children may initially be more likely to count in their first language. Gradually model the counting in English and the mathematical language such as 'more than' or 'less than'.

Extension activities

1. When the children are confident in counting, introduce some simple ways of recording the items that have been counted. Recording numbers can include the use of a simple tally system where one mark represents one item, or a drawing of each item which is then glued onto a bar chart. From the finished graph the children will be able to see if there are more or fewer or the same number of conkers, acorns or sycamore seeds. Use the bar chart to help with counting. The children could also use the computer to make tallies.

Key vocabulary

Number names up to 5, then 10 and then 20. Mathematical language such as count, how many, same as, less than, more than. Autumn words such as sycamore seeds, acorn, oak tree, conker and horse chestnut.

Links with the Early Years Foundation Stage curriculum for problem solving, reasoning and numeracy

Show an interest in number problems. Use some number names and number language spontaneously. Compare two groups of objects, saying when they have the same number.

Shape

 Activity name: *Three Billy Goats Gruff*

Objectives

To develop an interest in shape through play.

To recognise some familiar shapes.

To learn the names of some familiar shapes.

Use positional language.

Use size language.

Materials and preparation

A copy of *Three Billy Goats Gruff*. A Big Book and a dual-language text if possible. This activity is based on the story of the *Three Billy Goats Gruff* but can be based on any of the children's favourite stories that lend themselves to the theme. A large selection of wooden blocks which enable the children to build and role-play relevant parts of the story. The greater the number and range of wooden blocks available to the children, the more they will be able to engineer and create imaginary situations. Good wooden blocks will have straight and curved edges and have a mathematical relationship to each other, such as the triangular shapes relating to the square. Organise the storage of the blocks so that the children can access them easily, store them safely and accurately with the square shapes in the container which has a picture of a square as well as the name. The children will also need three goats and a suitable troll from a small-world collection or ones made by the children.

What to do

1. Tell or read the story of the *Three Billy Goats Gruff* so that the children are familiar with the main points of the story. Encourage the children to join in with the phrase 'Trip, Trap, Trip Trap' as each of the three the goats cross over the bridge to reach the tasty berries on the other side.

2. Discuss with the children which aspects of the story they may like to re-create, such as the goats crossing the bridge and meeting the troll and the troll being tossed off the bridge by the biggest Billy Goat Gruff. As the goats cross the bridge pause in the story and discuss with the children how many goats are on each side of the bridge and how many more are needed to make two or three. Make sure the children are secure about the order of numbers before asking what comes before or after any particular number. If the story is acted out as it is told, this will help the children in their counting. Make sure that the story is not interrupted too many times as this will spoil it for the children.

3. Ensure that there is a large space on the floor for the children to use the wooden blocks. This space needs to be 'protected' from the other activities in the nursery.

4. Encourage the children to play with the blocks to create 'houses' for the troll and the Billy Goats Gruff, and a bridge. They will probably create other structures that add to the original story. On some occasions the children can work out that two triangles can be used to replace a square.

5. Without too much intervention, the practitioner can play alongside the children to model language for shape, position and measures such as 'longer, shorter, under, over, on top off' as the children play. The practitioner can also encourage the children to use familiar shape names such as square, circle and triangle.

6. Photographs can be taken of the children's constructions for later discussion and a display. The children find that digital or disposable cameras are great fun to use.

Extension activities

1. Using some simple shapes with which the children are familiar, encourage the children to look at their environment including the nursery building and everyday objects in the nursery to recognise and talk about the different shapes such as rectangular bricks or circular windows.

2. Record the children's findings by taking photographs or making drawings of familiar objects depicting the chosen shapes such as books that are square or rectangular shaped.

3. Play a game where the children group the drawings or photographs under the headings related to each shape, remembering to name the object and its related shape. Count the number of items under each shape heading.

4. Extend the activity by introducing other shapes and other sorting activities.

5. The children will also enjoy making their own pictures from shapes or recognising shapes in pictures that they have drawn.

Key vocabulary

Vocabulary from the story of the *Three Billy Goats Gruff*. Shapes – circle, triangle, square. Language for shape, position and measures such as longer, shorter, edge, corner, top, bottom, underneath, next to, beside.

Links with the Foundation Stage curriculum for problem solving, reasoning and numeracy

Show an interest in shape and space by playing with shapes or making arrangements with objects. Show an awareness of similarities in shapes in the environment. Observe and use positional language. Are beginning to understand variations in size.

Number recognition

 ## Activity name: Busy bikes

Objectives

To use number language in play.

To recognise number labels.

To use equipment for measuring time.

Materials and preparation

Bikes, number labels for bikes and parking spaces. Time measures such as egg timers or digital timers. Riding bikes outdoors is one of the children's favourite outdoor activities. It is helpful for sharing the use of bikes to measure the amount of time that each child is able to use a bike by the use of a simple time measure. Numbering parking spaces and then parking the correct numbered bike in its allotted space helps children to use numbers in a purposeful activity.

What to do

1. Discuss with the children why it is a good idea to take turns in using the bikes and the ways in which this could be achieved in an equitable manner. Some ways could involve restricting each child's use to 'three laps' or measuring the time for use by using a large 'egg timer' or other simple digital timer. When the method of measuring time has been agreed, make sure that all the children understand how to use the system.

2. With the children, make some large number labels that will need to be fixed to each bike. It may be helpful to the children if a colour code is also used to identify each bike as well as the number. The labels will need to be sturdy as the bikes are well used!

3. Take the children outdoors and discuss with them their suggestions for where would be a safe place to park the bikes. Help them to consider the amount of space required.

4. Make some number labels to identify the parking spaces or chalk or paint a number on the ground if there is a suitable surface.

5. Celebrate the new parking places by enabling the children to park the bikes in their correct places and checking to make sure that the numbers match and that each bike is correctly parked. Count the number of wheels when all the bikes are parked.

6. Implement the chosen system for bike sharing and provide adult support so that the children understand how to use the system properly.

Extension activities

1. Discuss with the children how other number labels can be used in the nursery, such as a number to indicate how many children can play in the home corner or use the sand at any one time.

2. With the children, make some appropriate number labels making the sign relevant to the appropriate activity. A photograph of the equipment or the children using the equipment is a good start. Some of the labels could be made by the children using the computer and then printing them in a suitable large size font.

Key vocabulary
Numbers for the number labels.

Links with the Early Years Foundation Stage curriculum for problem solving, reasoning and numeracy
Show an interest in number problems. Use some number names and number language spontaneously. Use some number names accurately in play.

Counting

 Activity name: Dizzy dinosaurs

Objectives

To recognise numerals.

To use number names.

To enjoy number rhymes.

Use positional language and size language in context.

Materials and preparation

Drawings and books about dinosaurs. Thin card to make the dinosaurs. A large illustrated copy of the dinosaur rhyme or other rhyme to be used. A recording of the rhyme.

What to do

1. New and traditional number rhymes are a very enjoyable way for children to learn how to count. They offer many opportunities for repetition and children soon learn now to count forwards and backwards. Children who have English as their additional language will probably have some counting rhymes from their first language that they can teach the other children. Choose some children's favourite number rhymes and use these as the basis for a large room display. Take the opportunity to use imaginative ways of painting, printing and making a collage together with other creative skills. A display can take several sessions to complete and it is helpful to sketch out the background and discuss the ways in which the children's work will be used.

    Some traditional rhymes for counting forwards include:

    'One, two buckle my shoe'

    'One, two, three, four, five, once I caught a fish alive'

    'One potato, two potatoes, three potatoes, four …'

    'This old man he played one, he played nick, nack on my drum'.

    Some traditional rhymes for counting backwards include:

    'Five green and speckled frogs'

    'Five currant buns in a baker's shop'

    'Five little ducks went swimming one day'

    'Ten green bottles'.

This activity will be based on a new rhyme:

Dizzy dinosaurs
5 dizzy dinosaurs bouncing up and down
1 got left behind looking for his crown.
4 dizzy dinosaurs looking very smart
1 was very hungry and stopped for a tart.
3 dizzy dinosaurs slowed for a rest
1 raced ahead wanting to be best.
2 dizzy dinosaurs decided to chat
1 fell asleep and that was that.
1 dizzy dinosaur felt all alone,
'What shall I do?' he said – 'I need a phone!'

2. Introduce the rhyme to the children on several occasions. Discuss with the children the different types of dinosaur that they may be familiar with such as tyrannosaurus rex, stegosaurus, brontosaurus, triceratops and diplodocus.

3. When the children are sufficiently knowledgeable about the rhyme and the names of some dinosaurs discuss with them the idea of having a large display in their room. Decide with them which types of dinosaurs will be included in the display.

4. Divide the display board into five sections each of which will depict the main group of dinosaurs as they diminish in number together with the dinosaur that has left the main group. If the display board is organised in this way there will need to be a total of 19 dinosaurs. The background for the display will be a good opportunity to include the ideas of the children and to use splatter painting or other large-scale painting techniques.

5. With the children, make 19 dinosaurs, if possible giving the dinosaurs some individual characteristics or distinguishing features so that the children can recognise which dinosaurs remain and which leave the main group. Use as many creative techniques as possible. Draw the children's attention to the detail in the rhymes as this will help them with their drawings.

6. The children might like to complete one grouping of dinosaurs at each session so that there can be discussion about what the dinosaurs did and what happened to one of them.

7. There will be many counting opportunities during the creative activities such as counting the buttons on the four dizzy dinosaurs who look very smart and counting the jewels on the crown belonging to the dizzy dinosaur who gets left behind. Take time to have plenty of discussion with the children and to listen to their ideas.

8. When the creative activities have been completed, put up the display section by section, helping the children to count the dinosaurs as they arrive on the display board. Also count how many are left as each dinosaur leaves the main group. Take the opportunity to use positional language such as 'underneath',

'beside' or 'on top of' as the display is organised. There will also be opportunities to use size language when referring to big and little dinosaurs.

9. Frequently refer to the display on different occasions so that the children have opportunities to count and to repeat any new vocabulary.

Extension activities

1. Use a counting rhyme that includes numbers 1 to 10. If the rhyme '10 green bottles' is used, then add interest to the display by making the bottles into characters perhaps using storybook characters or differentiating by having bottles of different shapes and sizes or bottles with different shaped tops.

2. Remind the children that when there are no green bottles left this is nought or zero.

3. Use another counting rhyme that can be illustrated or acted by the children.

Key vocabulary

Numbers 0 to 10. Dinosaur names. New words from the rhymes used. Names of colours. Names of shapes or story book characters if used.

Links with the Early Years Foundation Stage curriculum for problem solving, reasoning and numeracy

Show an interest in number problems. Use number names and number language spontaneously. Recite some number names in sequence. Count aloud in ones, twos, fives or tens.

Counting

 Activity name: Who lives in this house?

Objectives

To recognise and use numerals.

To recognise and use shape names.

To use size and positional language.

Materials and preparation

This display activity offers an opportunity to draw together several different mathematical themes within a large-scale creative activity. The activity will be completed over several sessions. Paper, card, paint and collage material will be required. Use as many colours, textures and creative techniques as possible.

What to do

1. Decide where the display will be put and with the available space decide how many houses can be created. Each house will need a front consisting of roof,

chimney, doors and windows and behind the door of each house will be the group of characters or animals to whom the house belongs. It is important to have sufficient time to discuss with the children the shapes and colours of the door and windows and, of course, the number to be given to each house and who lives in that house. Try to make some part of the house relevant to the characters or animals that live in the house. If one house belongs to Cinderella then the front of the house might be decorated with silver shoes offering a counting opportunity. Another house belonging to one of the 'Three Pigs' could have a straw roof. The house that belongs to the witch from the story *Room on the Broom* could have the frog, the bird, the cat and the dog sitting on the roof. The house belonging to the seven dwarves could have seven windows.

2. With the children create the background for the display which could be a street scene with trees and gardens and spaces for the houses on either side of the street. Think of other opportunities to include numbers such as a 30 mile an hour speed restriction sign. The children will be sure to have some inventive suggestions for the name of the street!

3. Begin to make one house at a time, hopefully ending up with at least six or seven houses for the street.

4. When all the houses are finished, put up the display with the children adding their comments to what they are seeing with regard to shape and number.

5. After the display has been put up and admired, sit with the group of children and enjoy a mathematical discussion such as which house has the largest front door or how many windows a particular house has or how many animals are sitting on the witch's house. Model the use of positional and size language as well as numbers.

Extension activities

1. Choose an item for counting that appears on several of the houses such as the windows.

2. Choose a method of recording the number of windows on each of the houses after the children have counted them. It could be a simple tally system with marks made within the outline of a numbered house or a bar chart with a window symbol placed in the appropriate column for each of the houses.

3. Play a game where the children have to say which house in the street comes after the witch's house or which house comes two before Cinderella's house.

Key vocabulary

Numbers chosen for each of the houses. Vocabulary connected with the characters chosen by the children. Size language such as big and little. Positional language such as behind or next to. Shape language such as square and circle.

Links with the Early Years Foundation Stage curriculum for problem solving, reasoning and numeracy

Show an interest in numbers and counting. Use some number names and number language spontaneously. Compare two groups of objects, saying when they have the same number. Show awareness of similarities in shapes in the environment.

Measuring

 ## Activity name: Best foot forward!

Objectives

To provide opportunities for comparison of size.

To use a non-standard unit for measuring.

Materials and preparation

Each child will need a shoe and thin card for tracing round the shoe. Materials to decorate the outline of each shoe. The story of *Cinderella* to be read or told. A dual-language text of the story if available or a Big Book copy.

What to do

1. Introduce the theme for the activity through the story of *Cinderella* emphasising the part of the story where the handsome prince tries to find the owner of the silver shoe which is of a very small size. Role-play this scene if the children are confident.

2. Ask each child and member of staff to bring one shoe to the group. Talk about the colours of the shoes and the different methods of fastening such as laces, buckles or Velcro. Count the total number of shoes.

3. Look to see if any of the shoes have a number which indicates the size of the shoe. If this is the case then gather together all the shoes with the same size number and help the children to decide if they are all of the same size. Then look for shoe sizes that are bigger and smaller. Ask the children to think about which shoes might be the same size, bigger or smaller than Cinderella's shoe. When the shoes are in different size groups, count the number and help the children to understand that the total in each group when added together forms the total number of shoes.

4. Decide who has the shoe which is the biggest and smallest in the group.

5. Each child has to draw round their shoe, cut it out, name it and decorate it in a way that they will be able to recognise it as their own. Each child will need two cut-out shoes.

6. When all the cut-out shoes are assembled, count how many there are and then ask the children to arrange them in ascending size order from the smallest to the biggest.

7. Repeat the activity arranging the second shoe in descending size order from the biggest to the smallest. If the cut-out shoes are made from card, these activities can be repeated on different occasions.

Extension activities

1. Use one of the cut-out shoes as a non standard unit of measure. Assist the children to measure with the shoe and record the measurements.

2. Measure objects in the room, such as the table, the welcome mat and perhaps the height of the children.

3. A simple way of recording the measurements made by the children is to draw the item to be measured and then for the children to write in the appropriate measurement using the shoe as a non-standard measurement.

4. When the children measure their height in 'shoes' they could make a drawing of themselves and then write on the front of their drawing their measurement.

Key vocabulary

New vocabulary from the story of *Cinderella*. Mathematical language such as more than, less than, same as, smaller than and bigger than. Language connected with shoe fastenings such as lace-up, buckles and Velcro.

Links with the Early Years Foundation Stage curriculum for problem solving, reasoning and numeracy

Show an interest in number problems. Use mathematical language in play. Compare two groups of objects, saying when they have the same number. Separate a group of three or four objects in different ways, beginning to recognise that the total is still the same.

Counting

 Activity name: Flippity flop!

Objectives

To practise counting from 1 to 10.

To count things that cannot be touched.

To enjoy number rhymes.

Materials and preparation

A large space preferably outdoors. A copy of the rhyme 'Flippity flop'. Many large hoops, at least one for each member of the group.

What to do

1. Introduce the rhyme several times before going outdoors.

   > Flippity flop, flippity flop, get ready now for 3 big hops
   > 5, 4, 3, 2, 1 go …
   > Pippety pip, pippety pip, get ready now for 6 big skips
   > 5, 4, 3, 2, 1, go …
   > Bumpety bump, bumpety bump, get ready now for 4 big jumps
   > 5, 4, 3, 2, 1, go …

   Make sure that the children understand the actions that go with hop, skip and jump.

2. Start the rhyme with the children joining in and change the number of hops, skips and jumps each time.

3. When the children are confident in saying the rhymes, encourage each of them to take turns in saying the rhyme and choosing the number of hops, skips and jumps.

4. On some occasions let one or two children lead the group by saying and acting out the rhyme so that individual confidence is built. The other children can join in.

Extension activities

1. Place several hoops in the available space. Inside the hoop place large numerals which indicate the number of hops, skips or jumps to be made.

2. Say one of the rhymes, leave out the number of activities to be completed and emphasise which action is to be carried out and at the end of '5, 4, 3, 2, 1 go …' the children run to a hoop and carry out the action according to the number inside in the hoop and then run back to base.

3. 'Bumpety bump, bumpety bump, get ready now for lots of jumps 5, 4, 3, 2, 1, go …'

4. This activity is not a race as those needing to carry out 10 jumps will take longer than those carrying out three jumps! Give praise for the correct number of actions carried out and the effort made.

Key vocabulary
Numbers 1 to 10, hop, skip and jump.

Links with the Early Years Foundation Stage curriculum for problem solving, reasoning and numeracy
Show an interest in number problems. Use some number names accurately in play.

Summary: key principles for developing problem solving, reasoning and numeracy skills

■ In order to support children's mathematical development they needed to enjoy a wide range of activities.

■ Mathematical understanding is consolidated through the opportunity to practise skills such as counting in as many different situations as possible.

■ Purposeful activities give children a reason for learning about number, shape or measurement.

■ Staff who model mathematical language accurately enable children to learn and use the correct language during their play.

CHAPTER 9
Practical activities for knowledge and understanding of the world

In this chapter practitioners will find a range of activities that enables children to find out more about their locality and in doing so to take responsibility for learning how to respect and care for their immediate environment. The Early Years Foundation Stage framework spans a wide range of criteria for the early learning goals covering aspects of plant and animal life, raising awareness of how things work, developing skills in information and communication technology (ICT), learning how to construct and to use tools correctly together with a deepening knowledge of different cultures, religions and beliefs. The website www.blss.portsmouth.sch.uk has a calendar which provides information about cultural festivals.

The children in the reception class of a rural infant school knew several ways of saying 'Good morning' as the morning and afternoon registers were taken. They could say 'Good morning' in French, Italian, German and English. Their usual teacher was away and a different teacher took the morning register. One of the children, Tobi, was sufficiently confident to respond to his name by saying 'Guten Tag'. Although the teacher was a little surprised, she praised Tobi for his language skills and this resulted in several of the children responding to their names in a variety of languages. The children pointed out the small display of flags linked to the different countries and some of the children recounted their holiday adventures in these countries. The teacher decided to introduce the children to the ways in which Japanese people greet each other. The children practised saying 'Konichiwa' and also found out more about how children in Japan would greet their teachers by bowing. Some of the children looked for Japan on the globe and found out what the Japanese flag looked like. They drew the flag and added this to the display. The teacher had used an unplanned learning opportunity to extend the children's cultural knowledge. They had enjoyed displaying their language skills to a different member of staff and were ready to learn more.

As with other aspects of the early years curriculum it is important to offer children first-hand experiences and to begin with aspects of this area of learning that are relevant to them. The children learning English as an additional language, together with their families, bring to the nursery a wealth of experiences that they may be happy to share with all the nursery children and staff, if they are given appropriate support and confidence. Through their contribution to the activities, the children develop an understanding of how their culture and background is respected and valued, leading to

(Continued)

great gains in their self-esteem and self-worth. Through using artefacts, books and listening to music and stories connected with different cultures, the children can learn and think about the differences and the similarities in the children and their families in their group. They are able to gain a developing understanding of cultural attitudes and values and have a positive outlook towards becoming young global citizens.

In this area of learning there are many opportunities for discovery and experiential learning but also learning through direct teaching. Practitioners need to teach the children to use ICT equipment safely and correctly and then support them in using the equipment in as many learning activities as is appropriate. They need to ensure that there is equal access to the curriculum for both girls and boys in all aspects including ICT, cooking, the imaginative play area and in the use of construction materials.

The website www.hitchams.suffolk.sch.uk from Sir Robert Hitcham's Primary School offers excellent support for promoting ICT skills in the Early Years Foundation Stage.

Carrying out a risk assessment of the use of the equipment needs to be part of the setting's procedures. In all visits out of the nursery, practitioners need to carry out a risk assessment by walking the route themselves and noting any particular features or places where extra care may be needed. These concerns need to be discussed beforehand with staff and children, encouraging the children to take some appropriate responsibility themselves. Be clear with the children about the behaviour required during the visit so that it is enjoyable and safe for everyone. Check the required staff ratios not only for the group on the visit, but also for the groups remaining in the nursery.

Practical suggestions for activities which support the development in this area of learning follow.

- Growing sunflowers
- Flutter by, butterfly
- Minibeasts
- Spiders
- My favourite weather
- Let's celebrate!
- Where's my nursery?
- Keeping warm.

Exploring the natural world

 Activity name: Growing sunflowers

Objectives

To take an interest in the natural world.

To observe plant growth.

To use gardening tools safely.

Materials and preparation

Sufficient sunflower seeds and flowerpots, ideally two seeds and flowerpots for each child. Gardening tools of an appropriate size. Pictures of sunflower paintings such as those painted by Van Gogh. Drawing and painting materials.

What to do

1. This activity will normally take place during the spring season when sunflower seeds are readily available and growing conditions are ideal.

2. Before beginning the planting process, discuss with the children what the sunflower seed will hopefully look like when the flowers are fully grown. Talk about the beautiful colours, the size of the actual flower and particularly their height. Use the pictures on the sunflower seed packet and also the paintings of Van Gogh. Good resources are available at www.vangoghgallery.com.

3. Discuss with the children what natural conditions are necessary for growth, such as water, warmth and food, and how these will be replicated in the setting.

4. Encourage the children to open the packet and to hold a seed in their hand so that they can look carefully and describe what they can see. It may be possible to have some other flower seeds available to enable the children to compare the sizes of the seeds.

5. It may be preferable for the seed planting to take place outdoors or in an area of the nursery where any spilt compost can be easily cleared away. If this happens, the children will be able to do this if they have access to appropriate cleaning materials such as a dustpan and brush.

6. Help the children to place some compost material in the plant pot and then to plant the seed taking notice of the instructions on the seed packet.

7. The second seed is planted just in case the first does not grow. If the children end up with two successful plantings, then one can be used as a present for a family member or be part of the nursery nature area.

8. When the seeds have been planted, the children need to attach a label to their plant pot with their name and the date the seed was planted. Place the plant pots in a place which will be away from the busy activities of the nursery but accessible to the children for watering.

9. Over the next few weeks encourage the children to take responsibility for looking after their plant and when ready to plant out the seed in the nursery garden.

Extension activities

1. Encourage the children to carefully observe the sunflower and to take an interest in its speedy growth.

2. Careful observation can lead to recording growth through measurement and then recording this growth. A simple way of measuring is to use a piece of string to measure the height at regular intervals and then to glue the string to long pieces of paper or to draw a line the same length as the string. Remember to date the measurement.

3. Other activities connected with careful observation can include watching to see how the sunflowers track the sun across the sky and then drawing a sunflower, looking carefully at the petals and other parts of the flower head.

Key vocabulary

Vocabulary connected with the tools for planting the seeds such as flowerpot, trowel, fork and compost. Vocabulary describing the colour and the different parts of the sunflower such as petal, stem, and leaf.

Links with the Early Years Foundation Stage for knowledge and understanding of the world

Show curiosity and interest in the features of objects and living things. Describe and talk about what they see. Describe simple features of objects and events. Show an awareness of change. Realise tools can be used for a purpose. Show an interest in why things happen.

Life cycles

 ## Activity name: Flutter by, butterfly

Objectives

To enable children to have an interest in the natural world.

To learn more about life cycles.

To recognise some familiar butterflies in the environment.

Materials and preparation

A book of commonly seen butterflies. Pictures, video, DVD or other means for the children to identify butterflies. Drawing and painting materials. A large size dice. A copy of *The Very Hungry Caterpillar* by Eric Carle published by Puffin Books. A Big Book and dual-language text if available.

What to do

1. Talk with the children to find out what they already know about butterflies. Most butterflies fly by day and have brightly coloured wings, start life as an egg and eventually emerge as a butterfly. With the help of photographs or drawings help the children to identify one or two butterflies such as the tortoiseshell butterfly or the red admiral butterfly. Discuss with the children some special identification marks that will help them to recognise a particular

species such as the predominant colour or particular markings on the wings. If possible take the children on a butterfly walk or caterpillar walk, depending on the time of year. If they are lucky enough to see a butterfly at rest or a caterpillar on a leaf, take a photograph or look for the identification marks so that the species can be named later. If there is a buddleia bush in the vicinity this is a very likely place to find tortoiseshell and red admiral butterflies as the scented lilac flowers attract many butterflies.

2. Discuss with the children the four stages in the life cycle. A simple chart showing the eggs laid on a leaf, followed by the change into a caterpillar or larva, to a chrysalis, cocoon or pupa and then 'finally' to a butterfly will help the children to understand the changes. Eggs are usually laid on leaves or flower stalks that are best suited to the needs of the caterpillar who needs to eat a great deal of food to sustain it during the non-eating cocoon phase. The cocoon contains the developing butterfly which emerges after a period of about two to three weeks. The butterfly pulls itself free when the cocoon splits and then settles on a twig or leaf for its wings to dry.

3. Role-play the butterfly wriggling out from the cocoon and taking its first flight.

4. Introduce the story of *The Very Hungry Caterpillar* by Eric Carle. Enjoy looking at the illustrations and discuss with the children the enormous amount of food eaten by the caterpillar. Differentiate the food eaten by the caterpillar in the story and the food likely to be eaten by a red admiral or tortoiseshell butterfly.

5. Using some thin card cut into different shapes encourage each child to draw the four stages of the life cycle of a butterfly: egg, caterpillar, cocoon and butterfly. Each child will also need a drawing of a leaf and the food for the caterpillar.

6. When all the drawings are completed, play a game where each number on the dice represents a particular aspect of the cycle:

    1 represents the leaf.

    2 represents the egg.

    3 represents the caterpillar.

    4 represents the food.

    5 represents the cocoon.

    6 represents the butterfly.

    The children will need to throw the dice in the correct order 1 to 6 so that the life cycle is properly represented. When the appropriate number is thrown, the children each take the relevant picture so that they finish with a completed life cycle.

Extension activities

1. Each child will need a small piece of paper or card that is folded in half.

2. Open out the card or paper.

3. Place a small blob of thick paint in the centre of the fold and help the child to fold the paper or card along the crease and then press firmly down.

4. Open up the paper or card to reveal a beautiful butterfly!

5. Some children may like to cut out the butterfly when dry and use it for a display or a mobile.

6. Some of the butterflies could have some distinguishing marks put on them when dry so that they resemble a particular butterfly such as the tortoiseshell or red admiral.

Key vocabulary

Leaf, egg, caterpillar, cocoon, butterfly. Vocabulary from *The Very Hungry Caterpillar* story, particularly the foods eaten by the caterpillar.

Links with the Early Years Foundation Stage for knowledge and understanding of the world

Show curiosity and interest in the features of objects and living things. Describe and talk about what they see. Comment and ask questions about where they live and the natural world. Talk about what is seen and what is happening. Show an interest in why things happen.

Exploring the environment

 ## Activity name: Minibeasts

Objectives

To interest children in their environment.

To encourage exploration of the environment.

To use equipment appropriately and in a safe manner.

Materials and preparation

Books, video or DVD material, photographs and drawings of a wide range of minibeasts that are likely to be found in the local environment. Drawing and painting materials. Thin card to make a book. Magnifying glasses, if possible one for each child. Bug-collecting equipment such as a 'Creature Peeper' or 'Bug Vacuum'. Temporary storage for the minibeasts such as a 'Bug Habitat'. A clipboard to hold the chart for recording finds. Digital or disposable camera.

What to do

1. Discuss with the children the different types of minibeasts that they have recently seen in their garden at home or in the nursery garden. Their suggestions might include worms, snails, spiders, beetles, caterpillars, ladybirds, woodlice, slugs and ants. Some of the children might be unfamiliar with the names of the minibeasts so take time to repeat the names and identify the minibeasts. As the names are mentioned refer to the pictures and books that are available or if possible to the actual minibeasts that have been collected earlier and temporarily stored in an appropriate container such as a 'Bug Habitat'.

2. As part of the discussion extend the children's thinking by encouraging them to think about the likely places in which they might find some of the minibeasts and why these places are ideal homes for the creatures. Talk about taking great care of the minibeasts, being careful not to tread on them or to handle them roughly. Explain that if the minibeasts are kept for a short time in the nursery the children must remember to return them to their original home.

3. Decide whether the minibeast hunt will be one only of observation and recording or one where suitable specimens are collected and temporarily stored in the 'Bug Habitat'. Encourage the children to share the use of the digital camera to record their findings. On their return to the nursery the children can download their pictures and print them out for later use. Decide how the minibeast hunt equipment will be shared between the children and ensure that the children know how to use it correctly.

4. Create a chart on which the findings will be recorded. A simple chart which has a picture, together with the names of the most likely to be found minibeasts will enable the children to record the findings using a tally system. Include minibeasts such as worms, spiders and snails rather than ants, as these will be easier for the children to count.

5. Ensure that the children are clear about any safety rules and know that when they return to the nursery they must wash their hands after handling the minibeasts. Explain why this is important. A small group of children each with a member of staff is ideal for co-ordinating the finding and recording of the minibeasts, together with any possible collection and storage.

6. During the outdoor minibeast hunt, encourage the children to think about the likely places to find the minibeasts rather than lead the children directly to the likely places. Frequently use the vocabulary connected with the names of the minibeasts and their homes. Take sufficient time for the children to observe the movements, to notice the hiding places and to have turns in using the equipment. It is better to observe carefully a few creatures rather than rush round to try to see everything on one visit.

7. On returning to the classroom remind the children to wash their hands and encourage them to share their findings. This could be through discussion, observation, showing the methods for recording what they saw, or looking at the pictures downloaded from the digital camera. Model appropriate use of vocabulary.

8. Use the books and other reference material to enable the children to find out more about what interests them about their minibeast. Encourage the children to draw and paint their minibeast and use these for a display together with any photographs. Some children may like to make models of the minibeast and these can be included in a table display together with the books. Include in the display the comments of the children about the minibeast or their habitats. Refer to the displays frequently to encourage conversation about the minibeasts. Remember to return any stored minibeasts to their original homes.

Extension activities

1. Make a group zig zag book using thin card folded back on itself in zig zag fashion. A book containing 10 sides is a useful size.

2. Decide with the children the names of 10 minibeasts that they will include in their book.

3. Draw on each page of the book a number from 1 to 10 and decide which creatures will appear on each page, for example, one worm, two spiders and three ladybirds. Assist the children in deciding who will take responsibility for each page. Draw, cut out and glue the creatures onto their correct page. Use positional language when discussing how the minibeast are to be arranged on each page.

4. When all the creatures have been drawn, give the children plenty of opportunities for naming and counting the minibeasts. Refer back to the likely hiding places of the minibeast and where the children found them during their minibeast hunt. Glue the drawings into the book and share it with all the children before adding the book to the display.

Key vocabulary
Minibeast names. Vocabulary connected with a description of the minibeasts such as size and colour. Equipment names.

Links with the Early Years Foundation Stage for knowledge and understanding of the world
Are curious and interested in making things happen. Describe and talk about what they see. Show an interest in ICT. Know how to operate simple equipment. Remember and talk about significant things that have happened to them. Show an interest in the world in which they live.

Exploring the natural world

 ## Activity name: Spiders

Objectives

To find out about the natural world through first-hand experiences.

To develop skills of observation.

To know how to gather information and use it to gain knowledge.

Materials and preparation

Collect books, videos or DVDs, photographs and pictures about spiders. Make sure that there is some information about spiders that the children are likely to see indoors and outdoors. Pictures or drawings connected with the traditional rhymes such as 'Little Miss Muffet' and 'Incy Wincy Spider'. Digital camera. Yellow card for a picture of the sun and a small umbrella. Creative and collage materials.

What to do

1. Talk with the children about any spiders they have seen. Some children who have lived overseas may be able to describe some spiders that are very different from those seen in this country. Using pictures or other visual material discuss with the children some simple spider facts such as spiders have eight legs, eight eyes and a body divided into two parts. Most spiders spin a web made from silk strands. They lie in wait for insects to be caught in their web.

2. Take the children outside and look for spiders and for spiders' webs. Webs can be more easily seen during the autumn months, when the early morning dew makes them look very beautiful. Take time for the children to look very carefully at the way in which the web is formed from spiral threads and radial threads. If possible, take some photographs of the webs with or without resident spider. The children can download the photographs and print some out to use in the display or to use as a resource for discussion.

3. On the children's return to the nursery use the resource material to see if more information can be gained about spiders or spiders' webs .

4. Introduce the rhyme 'Incy Wincy Spider'

   'Incy Wincy Spider, climbed up the water spout.
   Down came the rain and washed poor Incy out.
   Out came the sun and dried up all the rain
   And Incy Wincy spider climbed up the spout again.

5. Make a large sun from the yellow card and with the sun and the umbrella act the rhyme 'Incy Wincy Spider'. All the children carry out the actions that accompany the rhyme and one child holds up the sun and another child holds up the umbrella at appropriate times.

Extension activities

1. Introduce the nursery rhyme 'Little Miss Muffet' and repeat the rhyme with the children. Accompany the rhyme with appropriate actions and encourage the children to join in with the actions and then also with the rhyme.

2. Decide with the children which of the rhymes, 'Little Miss Muffet' or 'Incy Wincy Spider' they would like to use for a display. Have a large central character, either Incy Wincy or Little Miss Muffet, and use collage techniques to make the display. Add other illustrative material relevant to the rhyme. Add any photographs that the children previously took. Put a large copy of the relevant rhyme on the display board and refer to it when saying the rhyme.

Key vocabulary

The vocabulary used in 'Incy Wincy Spider' and 'Little Miss Muffett'. Some names of spiders commonly seen such as the garden spider, house spider or money spider.

Links with the Early Years Foundation Stage for knowledge and understanding of the world

Comment and ask questions about where they live and the natural world. Show curiosity and interest by facial expression, movement or sound. Show an interest in ICT. Show an interest in the world in which they live.

ICT

 Activity name: My favourite weather

Objectives

To enable children to become familiar with using digital cameras.

To encourage an awareness of using other technological equipment.

To encourage observation skills.

Materials and preparation

A digital camera, computer and printing equipment to download and print photographs. Books connected with weather.

What to do

1. Begin the work on this topic by discussing with the children what words they could use to describe the weather today. Take the children outside and see if they have any other words or comments to describe the weather. Link the weather to the season if the weather is typical such as snow in winter or April showers in spring. Discuss with the children their favourite type of weather and the activities they like to do in this weather.

2. Discuss with the children what other words can be used to describe weather such as, windy, snowy, icy, foggy, cloudy.

3. Use the 'Welcome time' at the beginning of the session to practise phrases such as ' What's the weather like today?' and modelling the phrase 'Today it is ... '

4. Explain to the children that they are going to observe and record the weather for the week Monday to Friday and that they will do this by taking photographs of the weather. Make sure that the children know how to use the equipment, take the photograph and subsequently know how to download, choose and then print out the photographs. Take time to help the children understand the correct language for the equipment and for the activities such as 'download' and 'print'.

5. Draw up a rota with the children to show who will take the photographs on each day and normally at specific times such as morning, lunch time and just before home time. Of course, if there is a sudden weather event such as a snowstorm be ready to take additional photographs! Ensure that the children help with drawing up the rota recognising their name and the days of the week.

6. When the photographs have been taken, help the children choose which photographs are most relevant by viewing them together round the computer. There are probably other aspects of the photographs that are useful, so save and note these for future activities. Use the books to look for similar weather conditions and any associated activities such as building snowmen during winter snowfalls or putting on sunscreen before going out to play during hot, sunny weather.

7. When the photographs have been chosen they need to be printed and displayed under the relevant day of the week. Add relevant weather words together with speech bubbles of the children's comments. There should be many opportunities to use the new weather vocabulary either during the 'Welcome time' or in reference to daily weather conditions.

8. Instead of a display, an electronic book could be compiled from the downloaded pictures.

Extension activities

1. Introduce weather rhymes and use these as a basis to extend the weather display. The rhymes can also be used as the basis for action rhymes.

    The sun has got his hat on!
    Hip, hip hip, hooray,
    The sun has got his hat on and is coming out today!

    or

    Rain, rain, go away,
    Come again another day.

    or

    I hear thunder, I hear thunder;
    Do you too? Do you too?

Pitter, patter, raindrops,
I'm wet through
Are you too?

or

This is the way we jump in the puddles, jump in the puddles, jump in the puddles,
This is the way we jump in the puddles,
Jump, jump, jump.

Key vocabulary

Weather words such as windy, snowy, icy and cloudy. Phrases to describe the weather. Words associated with the equipment names and usage such as 'switch on and switch off'.

Links with the Early Years Foundation Stage for knowledge and understanding of the world

Show an interest in ICT. Know how to operate simple equipment. Show an interest in why things happen. Describe and talk about what they see. Talk about what is seen and what is happening. Show an interest in the world in which they live.

Valuing diversity

 Activity name: Let's celebrate!

Objectives

To introduce children to a range of cultures through practical activities.

To find out more about different languages, dress and customs.

To value the knowledge and skills of children and their families from a range of backgrounds.

Materials and preparation

Decide on the festivals that be will explored and celebrated, preferably choosing those that are relevant to the various cultures represented by the children in the group. Planning ahead on a yearly basis will enable many different festivals to be celebrated at the appropriate times of the year. The children and their families will be able to offer a range of resources relevant to the chosen festivals. Books connected with the festival. Video material or DVDs showing how festivals are celebrated such as the *Child's Eye View of Festivals* published by Child's Eye Media Ltd. Card and creative materials including poster paint and rice paper for the class book. Artefacts and other resource material to set up the imaginative play area for the children to re-create the celebration and to take part in the linked creative activities.

What to do

1. Decide on the festivals to be celebrated and begin to collect resources and to contact 'guest speakers' before the project begins. In this example the festival

of Children's Day in Japan is celebrated, but the ideas for the celebration can easily be applied to other cultural celebrations. Preparation for the festival and researching the background may need to take place over several weeks.

2. Invite family members or members of the local community to come into the nursery to talk with the children about how the festival is celebrated in their family. Children's Day in Japan is celebrated on 5 May and is known by the name – 'Kodomo no hi'. Festivals are known as 'matsuri'. Encourage the guests to bring in artefacts connected with the festival and photographs of the celebration taking place.

3. If possible show the children a relevant video or DVD of the celebration. This will support the children in their role play and give them ideas as to how to develop their play.

4. Organise a range of background activities to support the role play. Encourage the children in the group to lead some of the activities which can include the following.

   (a) Counting to 10 – 'ichi, ni, san, shi, go, roku, shichi, hachi, ku and ju'.

   (b) Useful phrases: 'Yes' – 'hai'. 'Thank you', – 'arigato'. 'Hello' – 'konnichiwa'. 'Goodbye' – 'sayonara'.

   (c) Finding where Japan is on the globe and finding out the names of the different islands – Hokkaido, Honshu, Shikoku, Kyushu.

   (d) Reading or telling stories such as *A Carp for Kimiko* by Virginia Kroll.

   (e) Learning about some cultural activities such bowing when meeting people, removing shoes when entering a building, using chopsticks to eat a meal.

   (f) Carrying out some practical activities such as simple origami. Origami is the Japanese art of folding paper into objects without cutting or gluing. 'Ori' means folding and 'gami' means paper. The children can also make a Japanese garden using a tray or plate, gravel, large stones for rocks and some aluminium foil for a pond. Look at pictures of Japanese gardens for some inspiration as to how to arrange the garden.

5. Discuss with the children how the imaginative play area could be set up to celebrate Children's Day and what artefacts should be in the area. Remind the children what they could involve in their play such as removing their shoes before entering the area. When appropriate use the digital camera to record the celebration and role play.

Extension activities

1. Make a class book to record the knowledge and skills that have been developed by celebrating the festival. Make a collage of the national flag to begin

the book. The Japanese flag is a red circle depicting the sun on a white background.

2. Include photographs of the role play connected with the celebration and any work of the children, such as origami or drawings and paintings connected with the story *A Carp for Kimiko*.

3. Another use of the digital photographs of the role play is to insert the photographs into a Word document and then add the comments of the children by either scribing for them or encouraging them to word-process their own comments.

4. Some children may like to copy some examples of Japanese calligraphy using a thick brush and white paint on black paper. Ask family members for examples of Japanese calligraphy.

5. Include some examples of 'Gyotaku' in the book. Gyotaku is the Japanese art of fish printing. Cover a washed and dried flat fish with a coat of poster paint. Place some rice paper on the fish and press firmly over the body of the fish. Gently take off the rice paper and leave the fish print to dry.

6. Use the book to enable the children to talk about their culture and for all the children to reflect on the activities that were connected with the festival. Over a period of a year the children could make many celebration books that will form a valuable resource for all the children.

Key vocabulary
Vocabulary connected with the chosen language and festival.

Links with the Early Years Foundation Stage for knowledge and understanding of the world
Show interest in different occupations and ways of life. Show an interest in the lives of the people familiar to them. Show an interest in the world in which they live. Describe significant events for family and friends. Gain an awareness of the cultures and beliefs of others.

Our environment

 ## Activity name: Where's my nursery?

Objectives

To enable the children to find out more about their local environment.

To learn vocabulary connected with direction and location.

Materials and preparation
A selection of maps showing the local area. Card for making a map. Play maps. Books connected with nearby facilities. Small-world equipment. Construction blocks.

What to do

1. Begin the discussion by talking with the children about their local environment, about where the nursery is and other places that might interest them such as the shops, the park, the library, the swimming pool and the playground. If possible have some photographs of these places and ensure that the children know the names of the places.

2. Show the children the selection of maps and help them to point out the location of the nursery. If possible show the children where their home is and discuss with them how they travel to nursery. If the distance from the nursery to school is not too great, trace their journey using a finger. Model the use of vocabulary such as turn right or left or straight ahead. The children may travel to school by bus, car, taxi or walk and can refer to some of the places that they see on their journey.

3. If possible take the children to visit a nearby place of interest that they have first located on the map and worked out their route to it. Take time for the children to look at the environment, to comment on what they see and to ask questions about what they see.

4. On returning to the nursery, make a simple map with the nursery at the centre of the map and the main roads and the areas where the children live.

5. Working with this map on the floor help the children to draw in some of the main features of the area. If possible locate the children's homes and let them walk their finger from their home to the nursery, talking about directions and the places of interest that they pass. When the map is completed it may be possible to display it on a more permanent basis so that the children can use it in their play. Make sure that any relevant books are placed nearby for the children.

6. Invite a 'guest speaker' such as the librarian to the nursery to talk about what happens at the library.

Extension activities

1. Make available the construction equipment and either the map made by the children or a commercially produced play mat or road mat. Small-world people and the play maps will encourage the children to create their own environment. Sensitively join in with the children's play to model appropriate vocabulary.

Key vocabulary

Vocabulary connected with local facilities such as park, playground, shops, school, doctor's surgery, library, church, temple, mosque. Vocabulary connected with direction and travel such as left, right, straight ahead, bus, road.

Links with the Early Years Foundation Stage for knowledge and understanding of the world

Show an interest in the world in which they live. Feel a sense of belonging to own community and place. Comment and ask questions about where they live and the natural world. Notice differences between features of the local environment. Investigate various construction materials. Join construction pieces together to build and balance.

Seasons

 Activity name: Keeping warm!

Objectives

To develop an interest in the natural world and the seasons.

To teach children the vocabulary connected with outdoor clothing and cold weather.

Materials and preparation

A large box ready to put in several examples of coats, hats, gloves and shoes. Have examples of the clothes in different colours. Materials relevant to the chosen season, in this example relevant to winter, for the decoration of the box such as using cotton wool for snow, silver paper for icebergs, penguins at the South Pole. Books connected with the chosen season.

What to do

1. Discuss with the children how they would like to decorate the large box, perhaps based on a snowy theme or a cold weather activity. Any season can be chosen and the clothing and decoration of the box altered accordingly. Keep the choice of season appropriate to the time of year. Look at the relevant books to find out more about the season.

2. Agree with the children how the decoration of the box will take place and who will do what.

3. Collect the items to decorate the box and organise the group activity.

4. Place the items in the box telling the children the names of the items as you do so.

5. Make up a very short story about children getting ready to go outside to play using the children's names in the story.

6. Emphasise the name of the item and the colour of the item.

7. As the story is told, invite one child at a time to reach into the box to find the appropriate item linked to the story.

8. After the story ask one of the children to help by collecting the items and placing them back in the box.

9. Play a game … 'Where's the green hat?' and so on. Use the same sentence structure.

10. Encourage each child to find the item and model the reply 'I've found the green hat'.

Extension activity

1. The children will need a folded pile of their own clothing in front of them.

2. Check to see if the children know and can say the names of each item of clothing.

3. Discuss with the children if it is helpful to put on some items before the others. Ask them to think if it would matter if they put their gloves on first!

4. When they hear you say the word 'Green for go', they start to put on their coat followed by hat, then shoes and finally gloves.

5. If they hear you say 'Red for stop' they must stop until they hear 'Green for go' when they can continue.

6. When all the clothes are worn correctly the child sits on the floor with their hands held up high!

7. Encourage the children to take turns in 'leading' the game by calling out 'Red for stop', or 'Green for go'. This will help to develop confidence.

8. 'Keeping cool' – This activity could also be played with a change of story and clothing suitable to the summer months.

Key vocabulary

Coat, hat, gloves, shoes, red, green and other colours connected with the clothes. Vocabulary connected with the chosen season. Repetition of vocabulary such as snow and cold in the story will help the children understand their meaning.

Links with Early Years Foundation Stage for knowledge and understanding of the world

Show an interest in the world in which they live. Describe and talk about what they see. Talk about what is seen and what is happening.

Summary: key principles for developing knowledge and understanding of the world

■ The children learning English as an additional language, together with their families, are a valuable resource to broaden the experiences of all the children in the nursery.

■ Experiencing aspects of various cultures helps all children to respect differences and to understand what can be shared in common.

■ Learning about the local environment and features of the natural world encourages children to be responsible and to take care of the places where they live and play.

In this chapter practical activities are included which support the development of physical skills together with ideas as to how children can learn more about nutrition and the benefits of enjoyable exercise. There is a need to encourage them in developing attitudes towards activity which will remain with them throughout their lives. Young children need to be active and involved in their learning as this is one of the ways in which they learn most effectively. Some settings will be well equipped with regard to the provision for physical activities, while other settings may have restricted outdoor space or few pieces of large-scale equipment. However, there can be many activities where children can be physically active without using large-scale equipment such as while moving to music, using musical instruments, or moving to accompany action rhymes or stories. Parachute games and using bats and balls in inventive ways are simple ways of encouraging physical activities.

If practitioners do not feel confident in having many children very active in a large area, it is best to start with a small group of children who know beforehand what the physical boundaries are and what the safety guidelines are which enable the children to move safely and to enjoy the activity. Start the session with a simple walking, hopping or skipping activity with many 'stops'. In this way the children will become familiar with listening carefully for direction and be ready to stop when required. When children use large-scale equipment, the practitioner needs to create a supportive atmosphere where children are encouraged to try new challenges but are sufficiently confident in themselves to know that a particular activity is, at that moment, something for which they are not yet ready. In any session, have one activity that is more challenging than the others and make sure that there is a member of staff near this piece of equipment to support and encourage the children. If staff break down a new skill into small achievable tasks, confidence is built and progress is made. Sometimes there is a need for staff to teach children who do not have hand–eye co-ordination new skills such as throwing and catching. Remember to praise effort and the willingness to try something new rather than just praising success. Do not expect instant success! An encouraging phrase in the children's first language will help them to make progress. Children requiring additional support can be encouraged to join in with activities, particularly when the children use equipment in open-ended ways and there is plenty of space for children in wheelchairs with staff available to provide support.

Children learning English as an additional language can often demonstrate their skills to the other children in the group as many of these activities are not dependent on English language proficiency. Making progress in physical activities contributes significantly to the development of self-esteem and confidence of all children. Their facial expression after persevering and achieving a new skill is undoubted proof of this.

Carrying out risk assessment is part of the practitioner's role and this is particularly the case when organising activities outdoors. Before the children go outside one member of staff should

(Continued)

go out to check the area for unwanted items and carry out a safety check such as looking for splinters or faulty equipment. Ideally, children should have access to outdoor play and learning for the majority of the day, which requires staff to be appropriately deployed. The children can also be taught to take an appropriate role in keeping safe by learning about how to approach and use equipment safely and in developing awareness about how to move safely among other children at different speeds and in a variety of directions.

This area of learning also includes helping children to understand the benefits of healthy eating and a healthy lifestyle and have an awareness of their own needs with regard to nutritious foods, rest and exercise.

Jean Jacques enjoyed the reception class topic on healthy eating. He particularly liked the afternoon when he and the other children looked at each other's teeth and heard from their special visitor about how he could brush his teeth properly. He carefully coloured in the drawings of the different types of teeth that the visitor brought with her. At the end of her visit she read a story about the wibbly wobbly tooth that Li had. Although he could not understand every word of the story, he knew what the story was about from the illustrations and also because he had taken the story home the previous day and had shared it with his mother. He liked listening to the story with the other children and being able to say 'wibbly, wobbly'.

Jean Jacques's teacher had obtained a dual-language copy of the story The *Wibbly, Wobbly Tooth* by David Mills, published by Mantra Lingua. She had asked Jean Jacques's mother to read the story to him in French and to talk with him about how to care for his teeth in preparation for the visit of the hygienist to his class. In this way Jean Jacques enjoyed the activity and joined in with the laughter of the other children as they suggested what should be done with Li's wibbly, wobbly tooth.

Practical suggestions for activities which support the development of physical skills follow.

- Penguins
- A busy, busy week
- Five of the best!
- Let's explore
- Look at what I can do!
- Toot, toot!

Action rhymes

 ## Activity name: Penguins

Objectives

To enjoy movement and gesture to accompany rhyme.

To move safely within the available space.

To develop confidence in physical activity.

Materials and preparation

A copy of the rhyme 'Penguins'. A recording of the rhyme. Pictures of penguins. Books about penguins and Antarctica. A video or DVD about penguins so that the children can see the range of penguin movements and learn more about how and where they live. Small-world equipment relevant to play activities based on 'Penguins in Antarctica'. White plastic milk containers.

What to do

1. Introduce the rhyme 'Penguins':

   > 10 smart penguins standing tall and sleek
   > With a black and white body and a bright yellow beak.
   > 1 felt hungry and looked for fish to eat,
   > Waddled off to the sea looking for a treat!
   > 9 smart penguins standing tall and sleek … continue the rhyme until there are 0.

2. Ensure that the children understand the rhyme together with the main descriptive features and actions of the penguin. Talk about the names of some penguins such as Emperor penguins, King penguins, Chinstrap penguins or Adelie penguins. If there are pictures of these penguins available, look for their distinguishing features and help the children to notice the differences. Talk with the children about how penguins live in Antarctica, what they eat and how they huddle together to survive the coldest winters on earth. Use the globe to find out where Antarctica is. Some children may be able to talk about seeing penguins at the zoo or on television.

3. Invite the children to suggest relevant actions for each line such as:

   10 smart penguins standing tall and sleek – stand up very tall with head held high.

   With a black and white body and a bright yellow beak – with two hands make a rounded body shape followed by a beak shape near the nose.

   1 felt hungry and looked for fish to eat – one hand rubs the tummy and then shades the eyes looking from side to side as if looking for fish.

   Waddled off to the sea looking for a treat! – waddle away with a bright smile thinking of the fish!

4. Repeat the rhyme several times and agree with the children what actions will be used. Model these together with the rhyme. An illustrated copy of the rhyme will be of help to some children. Discuss how important it is to move into a space and not to bump into other penguins that are on the move!

5. Initially act out the rhyme as a group before repeating the activity when one penguin will leave the main group as in the rhyme. Remember to start the rhyme at the appropriate number according to the number of children in the group.

6. Make the recording of the rhyme available to the children so that they can listen at any time.

Extension activities

1. Discuss with the children how the water tray could be adapted for small-world play with penguins. Ideally some 'penguins' and 'fish' are needed together with some large stones for the penguins to rest on. Some ice cubes added to the water will enable children to learn about ice and how it melts in warmer water. White, plastic milk containers can be weighted down to resemble icebergs. Further learning could be introduced with regard to floating and sinking.

2. Set up the water tray and ensure that the children are aware of the books and video or DVD of penguins and their habitat. These provide a resource for the children's play and language learning.

Key vocabulary

Vocabulary contained in the rhyme. The names of some species of penguins. Vocabulary connected with the actions which accompany the rhyme.

Links with the Early Years Foundation Stage curriculum for physical development

Respond to rhythm, music and story by means of gesture and movement. Move freely with pleasure and confidence. Move spontaneously within available space. Be able to stop. Manage body to create intended movements. Combine and repeat a range of movements.

Action rhymes

 Activity name: A busy, busy week

Objectives

To enjoy movement connected with rhymes.

To move spontaneously.

To develop confidence in physical activity.

Materials and preparation

A copy of the rhyme 'A busy, busy week'. A recording of the rhyme. Cards which help children to remember the different days of the week. Thin card and drawing materials to illustrate the rhyme.

What to do

1. Introduce the rhyme. Start off by reminding the children of the correct sequence of the days of the week and then say one line at a time echoed by the children repeating the same line.

A busy, busy week!
On Monday I can mix a cake.
On Tuesday I swim across a lake.
On Wednesday I jump up and down.
On Thursday I quickly march to town.
On Friday I kick a large, red ball.
On Saturday I stand up very tall.
On Sunday I like to say … hip hip hooray!
Then sit down ready for another day.

2. When the children can say the rhyme with support, discuss with them what actions they could do to accompany the rhyme. For this rhyme encourage the children to decide for themselves what actions they will be doing on an individual basis.

3. After several repetitions of the rhyme invite the children who want to, to demonstrate to the other children what they have decided to do for a particular day of the week. When the children are more confident, support them in saying the line or part of it. Change who acts out each line so that the children experience the actions and language connected with all of the lines.

Extension activities

1. When the children are very familiar with the rhyme, discuss with them the sequence for the days of the week and make some cards with a day of the week written on each card. If the children are confident in knowing the sequence, play a short game such as 'Which day comes after Wednesday?', which day comes after Friday?'. Make the cards as attractive as possible using a range of creative activities such as splatter painting for the card background or decorating the initial letter of each weekday.

2. Seven more cards of the same size and shape are needed. Help the children make a picture with the main object associated with each weekday. A digital photograph could be very appropriate for illustrating Wednesday, Thursday, Saturday and Sunday. Use the children's suggestions and these may include:

Monday – a cake

Tuesday – a lake

Wednesday – a child jumping up and down

Thursday – the buildings associated with the area in which the children live

Friday – a red ball

Saturday – a child stretching up very tall

Sunday – a child sitting down.

Key vocabulary

Vocabulary from the poem including the main rhyming words, cake and lake, down and town, ball and tall, hooray and day. The days of the week.

Links with the Foundation Stage curriculum for physical development

Move spontaneously within available space. Manage body to create intended movements. Combine and repeat a range of movements.

Healthy eating

 ### Activity name: Five of the best!

Objectives

To introduce the key components of a healthy lifestyle.

To encourage children to eat fruit and vegetables.

To find out more fruit and vegetables used in different cultures.

Materials and preparation

A range of fruit and vegetables to taste. Books illustrating fruit and vegetables used in recipes from different cultures. Large pieces of paper. Paper plates. Magazine pictures and drawings to cut out.

What to do

1. Discuss with the children the key aspects of a healthy lifestyle, including eating nutritious foods, having sufficient rest and exercise and maintaining good hygiene. Discuss how healthy food and proper rest and exercise contribute to building strong bones and enable the body to fight infection. Talk about why water is available in the nursery for the children to drink.

2. Invite the children to contribute from their own lives examples of a healthy lifestyle. Be sensitive to different family lifestyles.

3. Divide a large piece of paper into two columns, with one column having a smiley face and the other column having a sad face.

4. Encourage the children to make suggestions of healthy and less healthy foods. Be sensitive to the fact that the children may have a restricted choice of food. From all the suggestions ask the children to take it in turns to draw a picture of some obviously healthy and less healthy foods in the appropriate column. As the pictures are drawn, emphasise the names of the foods and encourage the children to repeat these names.

5. Show the children the collection of vegetables and fruits that have been assembled in the nursery. Name and describe these items and encourage the children to find some relevant pictures in the books and also match up the pictures from the magazines. Look at the colour and shape of the vegetables and fruit.

6. If possible, invite a parent or member of the local community into the nursery to describe how some of the fruits or vegetables are used in various cultural dishes. Perhaps during the celebration of Diwali a member of the Hindu community could explain how coconut is used in the preparation of sweets and snacks.

7. Depending on the facilities available, the children could assist in making a 'Fruit smoothie' from seasonal fruit, bananas, yoghurt and milk which are blended together. Another suggestion would be for a 'Berry surprise', again from seasonal fruit stirred into yoghurt. As with all cooking activities, remind the children of the need for good hygiene and safety when using equipment. Check for any allergies, particularly with nuts, or food preferences from a health, cultural or religious aspect. An alternative to dairy produce could be to use soya or goat's milk. When using berries the juice can easily stain clothes, so it is a good idea to make sure that the children's clothes are protected.

8. Support the children in cutting up small pieces of fruit and vegetables and organise a tasting session taking the time to name the items and to listen to the children describing the different tastes.

9. Provide some bowls of warm, soapy water so that the children can wash up the plates and other equipment.

Extension activities

1. Invite each child to choose a paper plate and several pictures from the magazines of different types of foods which illustrate healthy foods. Some children may like to draw and paint pictures from careful observation of the fruits and vegetables that they have been discussing and tasting. Arrange the pictures on the plate and encourage the children to name the items that they have chosen. Use positional language when discussing where the pictures will be placed on the paper plate.

2. Some of the fruit or vegetables could be used for printing and pattern making.

Key vocabulary
The names of the fruits and vegetables together with vocabulary which describes colour, size and taste.

Links with the Early Years Foundation Stage curriculum for physical development
Show awareness of own needs with regard to eating, sleeping and hygiene. Often needs adult support to meet those needs.

Action stories

Activity name: Let's explore!

Objectives

To enjoy movement which accompanies a story.

To move safely while working with others using large-scale movements.

To observe and imitate a range of movements.

To explore spatial relationships.

Materials and preparation

A copy of the story. A recording of the story. Equipment such as benches and tunnels to negotiate while on the journey. Creative materials for the display.

What to do

1. Introduce the story to the children. An outline of a suggested story follows.

The Treasure

One day two friends (use the names of the children) decided to go exploring in the jungle to look for a cave that had some treasure in it. They made their way through the tall grass carefully stepping over the twisty tree roots and bending low under the tree branches. They soon met two elephants who were plodding heavily through the grass and waving their trunks in the air.

'Where are you going?', trumpeted the elephants. 'We're going to the cave of the hidden treasure,' said the friends. 'Can we come with you?', asked the elephants. 'Yes,' said the friends and they all went along the path together. They walked slowly through some sticky, squelchy mud near the river and met some huge crocodiles swishing their long tails and opening wide their jaws.

'Where are you going?', hissed the crocodiles. 'We're going to the cave of the hidden treasure,' said the friends. 'Can we come with you?', asked the crocodiles. 'Yes,' said the friends and they all went along the path together.

They all tiptoed carefully along the edge of the lake when they saw some frogs jumping from rock to rock.

'Where are you going?', croaked the frogs. 'We're going to the cave of the hidden treasure,' said the friends. 'Can we come with you?', asked the frogs. 'Yes,' said the friends and they all went along the path together.

They all slithered and slipped along the path and rolled towards the trees when they saw some monkeys chattering excitedly and playing in the tree tops.

'Where are you going?', chuckled the monkeys. 'We're going to the cave of the hidden treasure,' said the friends. 'Can we come with you?', asked the monkeys. 'Yes,' said the friends and they all went along the path together.

The monkeys ran swiftly along the path and said, 'We will take you to the cave of the hidden treasure. Follow us and do exactly what we do.' The friends and all the jungle animals continued their journey, over the rocks, under branches, through tunnels and sometimes balancing on thin logs to cross very marshy areas. They all went round an enormous jagged rock covered with moss and then they saw the cave. Everyone thanked the monkeys and bent low to enter the mouth of the cave where they found the treasure. They danced round the amazing treasure and sang 'Let's share the treasure' which they did!

2. Make sure that the children are familiar with the story. Leave the recording of the story available so that the children can listen frequently. Use the story as a basis for the whole group carrying out the actions of all of the characters in the story. Through the actions help the children to understand the vocabulary connected with the actions together with the descriptive words which give further information about how the actions can be carried out.

3. Over time invite the children to decide who will take on the role of each of the characters and decide on an individual basis what actions will be used. Change the roles so that everyone has an opportunity to take on the role of the monkeys and lead the others in finding the treasure.

4. The treasure can be changed to suit each setting but could be a special story to be shared or some new construction equipment that the group can share and play with together.

5. When the children are confident in knowing the story, encourage them to join in, especially with the repetitive parts such as 'Where are you going?' and 'Can we come with you?' Probably the first spoken contribution to the story by the children will be to answer 'Yes.'

Extension activities

1. Create a large display choosing some sentences from the story for the children to illustrate. The children could choose an activity connected with the friends, the elephants, the crocodiles, the frogs, the monkeys and, of course, the treasure! Remind the children of the descriptive words that will help with the illustrations.

2. When all the creative work is completed, assemble the display. When the display is complete re-tell the story and use the display as a resource for further language work.

Key vocabulary

The vocabulary from the story especially the names of the animals, the action words and the descriptive words accompanying the actions. The vocabulary of the repetitive phrases.

Links with the Early Years Foundation Stage curriculum for physical development

Manage body to create intended movements. Combine and create a range of movements. Respond to rhythm, music and story by means of gesture and movement. Be able to stop. Move freely with pleasure and confidence in a range of ways, such as slithering, shuffling, rolling, crawling, walking, running, jumping, skipping, sliding and hopping. Judge body space in relation to spaces available when fitting into confined spaces or negotiating holes and boundaries.

Skills development

 Activity name: Look what I can do!

Objectives

To use a range of equipment in creative ways.

To improve co-ordination and develop specific skills.

Materials and preparation

A range of small-scale equipment such as balls of different sizes including foam balls, hoops of different sizes, skipping ropes, beanbags, bouncy balls to sit and bounce on, rope quoits, skittles, stilts and a basketball net of an appropriate height.

What to do

1. Decide on the choice of equipment depending on space available and number of children in the group. Carry out a safety check of the equipment and the area in which the equipment is placed. Ensure that the children are wearing appropriate clothing and footwear so that they are safe. Be sensitive to cultural and religious preferences. Involve the children in the organisation of the equipment and make sure that it is readily accessible and with sufficient space so that there is no crowding when the children collect and return the equipment.

2. Before the children use the equipment, check that they are clear about any signal that is used to stop any activity, that they know how to use the equipment safely and how to store the equipment correctly when it is returned. Depending on the space available it may be helpful to organise a particular space where each piece of equipment is used as this ensures that balls are less likely to interrupt other activities. The use of the space can be identified by a large laminated card placed appropriately which illustrates the equipment to be used.

3. Begin the session with some warm-up activities such as running and stopping, skipping hopping and jumping. Carry out these activities at different speeds and in different directions, encouraging the children to move into different spaces, always avoiding other children.

4. When the children have chosen their equipment encourage them to be creative in their use of the equipment. Initially some children may need some ideas such as:

    rolling the ball to strike a skittle

    placing a skipping rope on the ground and jumping from side to side

    jumping in and out of a hoop placed flat on the ground

throwing and catching a large foam ball with a partner

throwing bean bags into a hoop

using the bouncy ball to weave in and out of some skittles to follow a particular pathway.

5. Encourage inventiveness, effort and perseverance and of course safe practice. On some occasions invite one of the children to demonstrate a particular activity and, if there is sufficient equipment, make this into a group activity where all in the group imitate the action. Over a period of time encourage the children to use the whole range of equipment.

6. Finish the session by checking that all the equipment has been stored correctly and end with a traditional game such as 'Ring-a-ring of roses' or an action song such as 'Head, shoulders, knees and toes'.

Extension activities

1. When the children are using the equipment, practitioners should observe them carefully and note which children need some specific help with particular skills such as throwing or catching. Teach the skill which needs to be developed, checking that the equipment used is of an appropriate size and conducive to success. Always be encouraging and praise any small success and effort. Break down the activity into small actions and accompany the action with appropriate words which will help the children to remember what to do. Practise the skill but not for too long, and finish on a successful note.

Key vocabulary

The names of the equipment used. Vocabulary linked with actions such as hopping, skipping, quickly, slowly, left and right. Vocabulary from the traditional game or action song.

Links with the Early Years Foundation Stage curriculum for physical development

Move spontaneously within available space. Be able to stop. Show respect for other children's personal space when playing among them. Persevere in repeating some actions/ attempts when developing a new skill. Engage in activities requiring hand–eye co-ordination.

Using wheeled vehicles

 Activity name: Toot, toot!

Objectives

To demonstrate control of wheeled vehicles.

To improve co-ordination skills.

Materials and preparation

Large-scale wheeled equipment such as trikes, bikes, scooters, pedal cars. Cones, traffic lights, zebra crossing and other road layouts.

What to do

1. Discuss and agree with the children their ideas for sharing the wheeled equipment. This may be in terms of a number of laps or use of a simple timing device. When the method has been agreed, make sure that all the children understand how to use it and why it is important to use it so that all the children can have a turn. Initially it is helpful to the children if there is a member of staff to supervise this, after which one of the children could take responsibility.

2. Discuss the type of 'challenges' that are available and check for the safety of the equipment and that the clothing of the children will not get caught in the wheels. Make sure that the children understand the signal that will be used to stop the activity and agree the boundaries for the use of the equipment, especially if there is a very large area available. Explain the 'rules of the road' and ask the children why it is necessary for everyone to keep to these rules. Some vehicles could have numbers fixed to them which indicate where these vehicles are to be parked in the numbered parking areas.

3. Set up the area to enable the children to use the equipment as they wish or to try out the various 'challenges' that are available which could include:

   weaving in and out of the cones which are placed at intervals in a long line

   stopping at the zebra crossing and the traffic lights

   obeying the 'rules of the road' with regard to roundabouts or other aspects of the road layout

   parking correctly in the identified and numbered parking areas.

4. At the end of the session check that all the vehicles have been left in the correct place and praise and encourage safe use of the vehicles, appropriate sharing of the vehicles and occasions when the children were particularly aware of the needs of others.

Extension activities

1. Introduce some rhymes connected with travel such as 'My red pedal car'.

   Here I come in my red pedal car
   My red pedal car
   My red pedal car
   Here I come in my red pedal car
   Look at me, I'm going far!

or

> I can ride my bicycle,
> I bought it at the shop,
> When I see the light is red,
> I know I have to stop.
> When I see the light is green,
> I know that I can go.
> On the way, every day,
> Green means, 'Go'. (from the book *'Hippety- hop, Hippety- hay* by Opal Dunn)

Key vocabulary
Names of the wheeled vehicles. Stop, go. Directions such left, right, straight ahead, forwards and backwards. Vocabulary connected with the road layout such as zebra crossing and traffic lights. Vocabulary from the chosen rhymes based on travel.

Links with the Early Years Foundation Stage curriculum for physical development
Negotiate an appropriate pathway when walking, running or using a wheelchair or other mobility aids, both indoors and outdoors. Operate equipment by means of pushing and pulling movements. Observe the effects of activity on their bodies.

Summary: key principles for developing physical skills

■ Developing confidence in physical skills is closely linked to the development of self-confidence and self-esteem.

■ It is important for practitioners to praise the children's efforts and perseverance as well as celebrating the success they achieve.

■ Children can learn about and take an appropriate part in risk assessment activities.

■ Children enjoy being active learners and gain skills that will enable them to enjoy physical activity in the future.

Practical activities for creative development

The development of creativity in young children enables them to make connections between several areas of learning and in making these connections they are able to extend their knowledge and understanding. Creativity is a way of thinking and doing which is not restricted to artistic or musical ability. All children, and especially those learning English as an additional language, can use the whole range of creative activities to communicate and express their ideas. Through music, dance, role play and imaginative play they can develop confidence, share aspects of their culture and enjoy sensory and physical activities.

Music was an important part of school life. The reception children enjoyed singing nursery rhymes and action songs each day. They had enjoyed the story of the *Three Billy Goats Gruff* and were using the percussion instruments to accompany the goats as they trip trapped across the bridge. The children could choose to use the chime bars, the maracas, the tambourines or the triangles. One of the children energetically used the cymbals as the troll was butted from the bridge by the biggest Billy Goat Gruff. Once the musicians were confident in the timing and use of their instruments four of the children acted out the story. Hannah took on the role of the troll. Usually Hannah was a very quiet child who lacked confidence and had to be encouraged to start any new activity. However, she excelled in the role of the troll and used her own words as the troll informed each of the Billy Goats Gruff that they would be eaten! Her gestures and facial expressions aptly characterised the fierce troll. Hannah spoke out well and with confidence, and surprised everyone with her performance. Through the musical and physical activity Hannah demonstrated her skills and she knew that she was good at something and liked the praise from her teacher and the other children.

Supporting young children to become creative thinkers enables them to develop in all aspects of future learning including science and mathematics.

For children to develop their creativity they need practitioners who plan a nurturing learning environment where creative risk-taking is encouraged and experimentation is welcomed. Children need to know that their effort will be valued and respected even when the 'result' is not a polished 'end product'. Not all creative activity has to have an 'end product' and it is the creative process and the learning experience which is of value. Many practitioners will have had the experience of feeling that the children should always have something to take home at the end of

(Continued)

(Continued)

the day but know that this criteria is not necessarily the best way of planning and organising the children's learning. Children need time to work at their creation over a period of time. They need time to gain inspiration, research their theme, represent their ideas and to become confident, experimental thinkers. Parents can be kept informed of the effort their child is making, and of the ideas that they have through looking at photographs of 'work in progress'. This does not preclude practitioners and children constructing displays of the children's creations, as this is one way in which their creativity can be valued and shared. When displays are constructed the children's work should be shown in the best possible way using attractive materials in a prominent yet safe place. This does not in any way mean that adults add to the children's work to improve the look of it. Displays can be used as a resource to develop learning as part of the practitioner's planning for a particular theme or activity. Using appropriate backing paper, borders and fabrics, together with a collection of related artefacts for a display, adds to the children's creative work and enables them to have pride in what they have achieved. Over a period of time all the children's work should be part of a display not only those who complete their work to what an adult might describe as 'a completed end product of a high standard'.

The role of the practitioner is to support the creative development of all children, not only those who seem to possess natural creativity. By organising sufficient and imaginative resources together with a supportive environment, the children will feel confident to develop and extend their ideas, become lateral thinkers, tackle new challenges, and work as an individual and co-operatively as part of a group. In addition, the practitioner's role is to teach the children a wide range of techniques such as how to mix paints or how to carry out splatter painting. The children then use these techniques to develop their own unique creations demonstrating an individual and imaginative approach.

If space permits, an area of the nursery can be set aside for the 'Creative Workshop' where resources are readily accessible to the children and the opportunity to be creative becomes part of every nursery day. Excellent storage and organisation is the key to a successful workshop. Children need to know how to put away and store valuable resources and to be responsible for taking care of unfinished work that is stored in this area. Within this space, materials which provide a stimulus and inspiration for creativity can be displayed, with changes made according to current themes and the children's interests. Children, families and members of the local community from all cultural backgrounds may wish to share their artistic and musical heritage and broaden the experiences of the children and staff in the setting through contributing to resources and displays.

Practical suggestions for activities which support this area of learning follow:

- All my own work!
- Trip, trap. Trip, trap
- Welcome!
- Mix it up!
- Working together
- Let's investigate!

Using creative materials

 Activity name: All my own work!

Objectives

To offer children the opportunity to explore a range of creative materials.

To encourage children to use the materials in an imaginative and original way.

Materials and preparation

A wide range of creative materials including: feathers, beads, pipe cleaners, curly gift ribbon, lentils, rice, sand, fabrics, wool, string, sequins, leaves, pressed flowers and papers of different sizes, shapes, colours and textures. Card, and junk material for three dimensional (3D) models. PVA glue and spreaders. Aprons.

What to do

1. If possible, set aside a small area of the nursery for a workshop where the children can go at any time and use the materials as they wish. Remember to have some aprons available with the children knowing that the number of aprons is the same as the number of children who can use this area at any one time. Over a period of time introduce a small range of the creative materials. As the children become more proficient in using and organising their resources, extend the range of materials on offer. Within the nursery area, there needs to be an area where 'work in progress' can be stored safely as creativity takes time to come to fruition and the children may wish to return to their work as they think how they wish to develop it.

2. Within the workshop area a small display stand could be used to display the finished work for a short period of time. Before the children take their work home, a photograph should be taken and stored for the children to reflect back on their work at a future point. This display area should reflect the pride that everyone in the nursery has for the children's work.

3. When additional resources are added to the creative workshop, it is an opportunity to teach the children new skills in handling the materials appropriately. While working alongside the children, the staff have an opportunity to introduce vocabulary which best describes the materials such as shiny, soft, silky, rough, smooth, bumpy and fluffy together with the colours of the materials. Listen to the children's contributions and include these in the discussion.

4. In the workshop area it is useful to display materials that will help creativity. These need to be changed to maintain the children's interests and can include photographs and books of the natural environment such as a rainbow, a spider's web, the sunset, pressed flowers, or a rough sea. Music, artefacts and fabrics linked with different cultures also act as stimuli. Do not have too much

available at one time and use the resources as a focal point of discussion or a simple research activity such as finding out the names of some wildflowers and then learning how to press these ready for future creative work. It is important that the children can touch objects and use all of their senses in exploring an object. Explain to the children how to handle objects carefully and to respect items that are brought in from home.

5. As the children visit the area encourage them to experiment and explore and to create their own pictures and 3D models. Staff need to support the children in their choice of activities and to respect this choice without trying to dampen their creativity. Appropriate support enables children to acquire skills and then to use these in a way which expresses their creativity.

Extension activities

1. Cut out some picture frames of different colours, sizes and shapes. Have some thick card available which acts as the backing sheet for the picture. Leave these available in the workshop area along with a range of creative resources.

2. Encourage the children to create a picture within the frame by placing their chosen materials on the thick card. Then place one of the frames over the picture to create a finished piece of work. A photograph can be taken of a picture that the children find particularly pleasing. It is not always necessary to permanently glue the materials within the picture frame as many pictures can be created and then changed according to the children's preferences. Sensitive support may be needed from staff which enables the children to take the ideas and inspiration from the stimuli and to use these for their own creativity. This is best done by having a discussion with the children and listening to their ideas.

Key vocabulary
Vocabulary to describe the creative materials and the techniques used for the activity.

Links with the Foundation Stage for creative development
Explore colour and begin to differentiate between colours. Create 3D structures, Begin to be interested in and describe the textures of things. Respond in a variety of ways to what they see, hear, smell, touch and feel. Show an interest in what they see, hear, smell, touch and feel.

Making music

 Activity name: Trip, Trap. Trip, Trap

Objectives

To encourage creativity with musical instruments.

To explore sound made by percussion instruments.

Materials and preparation

A copy of the story of the *Three Billy Goats Gruff*. A selection of percussion instruments including drums, bells, cymbals, tambourines, triangles, chime bars and maracas.

What to do

1. Agree with the children the signal that will be used which tells them to stop using the instruments and to put them on the floor.

2. Invite the children to choose an instrument and to put it on the floor in front of them. Make sure that there are sufficient instruments for each child to play one.

3. Begin the session with some nursery rhymes which are sung and accompanied by the children using the percussion instruments. Practise the stopping signal several times and praise the children when this is achieved quickly!

4. Continue the activity, adding variety by choosing different nursery rhymes and having loud and soft accompaniment. Think about the rhythm in the rhyme and encourage the children to maintain the rhythm as they accompany and sing the rhyme.

5. Divide the children into smaller groups and support each group to choose a nursery rhyme which the other group is going to guess just from the rhythm. Guess the nursery rhyme just from the rhythm. When the correct rhyme has been guessed invite the group to sing and accompany the rhyme by themselves or possibly by an individual child who is confident. Initially the children will need a member of staff to lead each group activity.

6. Each group makes up a simple rhythm and this is copied by the other group. The children need to listen carefully so that this is done accurately. It can be helpful to clap the rhythm before using the percussion instruments.

Extension activities

1. Tell or read the story of the *Three Billy Goats Gruff* or any other story that lends itself to a re-enactment accompanied with percussion instruments. Remind the children of the agreed stopping signal.

2. When the children are familiar with the story identify key parts of the story that can be re-enacted with musical accompaniment.

3. Key parts of the story with suggestions for playing the percussion instruments could include:

    (a) The Three Billy Goats Gruff playing happily in the fields before deciding to cross the bridge to eat the juicy berries – the children shake the bells quickly and lightly.

    (b) The smallest Billy Goat Gruff starts to cross the bridge – the children play the maracas softly thinking of the rhythm, 'Trip, Trap. Trip, Trap'.

(c) The troll comes out of his house and asks the smallest Billy Goat Gruff where he is going – the children beat the drum quickly as the troll approaches the bridge.

(d) The troll allows the smallest Billy Goat Gruff to cross the bridge towards the berries – the children play the maracas, Trip, Trap. Trip, Trap.

(e) The actions are repeated as the middle-sized Billy Goat Gruff crosses the bridge – the children play the maracas in a louder manner, Trip, Trap. Trip, Trap.

(f) The big Billy Goat Gruff begins to cross the bridge – the children use the tambourine for a louder sound 'Trip Trap. Trip Trap'.

(g) This time the troll leaps onto the bridge and is butted off the bridge and into the water by the big Billy Goat Gruff – the children play the drum loudly as the troll leaps on to the bridge and then there is one clash of the cymbal as the troll falls, splash, into the water.

(h) The Three Billy Goats Gruff all play in the field eating the juicy red berries – the children shake the bells quickly and lightly.

If there are sufficient children in the group invite some children to act out the story while the other children play the percussion instruments.

Key vocabulary
The names of the percussion instruments and the descriptive words describing how the instruments are used such as shaken, beaten and struck. The chosen nursery rhymes. Vocabulary from the story of the *Three Billy Goats Gruff* and the phrases repeated by each of the characters in the story such as, 'Where are you going?'

Links with the Early Years Foundation Stage for creative development
Join in singing favourite songs. Show an interest in the way musical instruments sound. Begin to move rhythemically. Tap out some simple repeated rhythms and make some up.

Mark-making

 ## Activity name: Welcome!

Objectives

To introduce children to different ways of writing.

To encourage children to use different scripts in creative ways.

Materials and preparation
Collect examples of different scripts that children may have already seen in their local environment. Dual-language story texts containing different scripts. Card and creative materials. Materials for writing in the mark making area.

What to do

1. Discuss with the children what examples of different scripts they have seen. Some of the children may be able to write some words from their first language. Other children may be able to contribute examples from the writing used by members of their local community. If possible ask a parent, member of staff or a member of the community who use different scripts to show the children how they write and how the words are pronounced. If possible, record the words for future use by the children. The children could also listen to a recording of the dual-language story.

2. If it is not possible to find examples of other scripts from the children or parents there are some very useful websites that provide examples of different scripts. One website that gives examples of 'Welcome' in different scripts is www.bfinclusion.org.uk. Here you will be able to find examples of Urdu, Tamil, Nepali, Greek, Arabic, Russian, Punjabi, Japanese and many others.

3. Ask the children to look carefully at the different shapes and to think in what ways these scripts differ from the roman script used when writing English. Look for straight lines, curves and symbols that are specific to a particular script such as the beautiful hiragana symbol 'so' in the Japanese word for welcome. Remember that the print style may be very different, for instance the Arab script is read from right to left and traditional Japanese script is read from top to bottom. Children used to different print styles have to make some considerable adjustment to read English.

4. Discuss with the children how they would like to organise the mark-making area so that they could include different scripts in their mark-making activities. Involve the children in the reorganisation and make sure that there are plenty of examples of different scripts in the area. If possible use the scripts which are from the first languages of the children in the group and encourage these children to demonstrate the correct ways of writing the script.

5. Display the children's work. Look at the books that contain different scripts and, if possible, match some of the symbols written by the children with the text in the book. Encourage the children to learn the correct pronunciation of some of the words that they have written. Enjoy the story!

Extension activities

1. Decide on some key words that can be written in different scripts. If possible choose the scripts that represent the languages used by the children in the class or in the local community. Useful words could include: the names of the children, 'Welcome', the days of the week, numbers 1 to 20, or bilingual labels for the objects in the classroom.

2. Find out how to write the chosen words in the various scripts and encourage the children to write them very carefully so that they could be used in the

setting, perhaps as part of a 'Welcome' poster to be displayed in the entry. It may take some practice to get the script just right as the symbols could be very new to some of the children. If possible find some very special creative materials to use in this activity!

Key vocabulary

The vocabulary chosen from the different scripts.

Links with the foundation stage for creative development

Differentiate marks and movements on paper. Understand that they can use lines to enclose a space, and then begin to use these shapes to represent objects. Respond in a variety of ways to what they see, hear, smell, touch and feel. Differentiate marks and movement on paper.

Colours

 ## Activity name: Mix it up!

Objectives

To experiment with creative materials.

To explore colour through painting activities.

Materials and preparation

Yellow, red, blue paint (powder, block or liquid paint). Brushes of different thicknesses. Trays or palettes for mixing. Papers of different shapes, textures and colours. Artefacts of different colours. Photographs or pictures of a rainbow. Collage materials such as fabrics, feathers, sequins, buttons, beads, magazine pictures, wallpaper pattern books. PVA glue and spreaders. Card for the collage. Scissors.

What to do

1. Discuss with the children the names and colours of the artefacts. Check that the children know the names of other commonly used colours. Be sensitive to any children who may have colour blindness but be aware that this may just be that they do not know the names of the colours in English.

2. Invite the children to handle the artefacts such an orange, peas, coloured pencils or a banana. Where possible choose artefacts that can be handled to feel the texture and develop visual awareness and possibly enable the children to use their sense of smell. In this way the children can use many of their senses and extend their vocabulary when discussing the objects.

3. Discuss colour in nature and perhaps refer to the colours in the rainbow, which from top to bottom are red, orange, yellow, green, blue indigo and violet – the

colours of the spectrum. If rainbow colours are discussed, the children will need to see a photograph or drawing of a rainbow.

4. Discuss with the children how the primary colours, yellow, red and blue when mixed in the correct proportions form other colours.

5. If this is the first time that the children have taken part in this type of activity, it may be helpful to show the children some of the techniques. When mixing paint it is sometimes difficult for the children to lift the colour out of one palette into another in the correct proportions. This can be made slightly easier if the paints are on a flat surface such as a tray when the small amounts of paint can be dragged across with the paintbrush to form other colours. Emphasise to the children that it is preferable to work with small amounts of paint and that the darker colour should be added in very small amounts to the lighter colour. This will take plenty of practice and many black colours will initially emerge! The children will need plenty of time to experiment and enjoy this activity.

6. Set out the materials in the workshop area together with many different shapes, colours and textures of paper as well as junk modelling materials for the children who wish to make and paint some 3D models. Encourage the children to experiment with the paint, with staff ready initially to support the children with the techniques especially with the construction of the models.

7. A chart made by the children to remind them of some colour combinations would be helpful. Label the colours. Begin with the commonly used colours before thinking about more exotic colours. Use mathematical language such as more or less when discussing with the children how much of each paint is used.

    Yellow and a small amount of blue when mixed together form green.

    Yellow and a small amount of red when mixed together form orange.

    Yellow and red and blue when mixed together form brown.

8. The children will need plenty of time to experiment with the colours and may not wish to paint a picture. However, their successful paint mixing activities can be stored safely when dry and used within the workshop area for a small display. On other occasions a different display can be created from the children's work depicting one colour together with their models painted in the same colour and also the associated artefacts.

Extension activities

1. Make sure that all the collage materials and paint are accessible to the children and they know how to organise the materials and clear them away.

2. Discuss with the children what sort of collage they would like to make. The collage could be small and individual or for a larger group activity. The children may like to concentrate on one dominant colour or use a picture from

a well-loved book for their inspiration. A topical theme such as autumn or carnival could be linked to the collage. If a particular theme such as autumn is chosen, ensure that there are sufficient materials of the relevant colours available.

3. Staff can work with the children to model the vocabulary of colour and texture and assist with any technical difficulties. Remember to take some photographs of the children's work. Use positional language when discussing with the children where the different pieces of the collage material will be placed.

Key vocabulary
Vocabulary connected with colours and textures. Vocabulary connected with textures such as smooth, shiny and soft. Vocabulary linked to the paint mixing activities such as lighter or darker and more or less.

Links with the Foundation Stage for creative development
Create three-dimensional structures. Differentiate marks and movement on paper. Begin to be interested in and describe the texture of things. Explore colour and begin to differentiate between colours. Begin to combine movement, materials, media or marks.

Collage

Activity name: Working together

Objectives

To enable children to work together to explore and develop ideas.

To develop the ability to communicate ideas.

To use a variety of materials to create the collage.

Materials and preparation
A painting, photograph or book to provide inspiration and use as a basis to encourage experimentation and imagination when developing the children's ideas. In this activity the book *Fix it Duck* by Jez Alborough and published by HarperCollins is used. Some examples from other cultures or religious celebrations could also provide inspiration. Yellow, red, and blue paint. Trays or palettes for mixing. Brushes of a variety of thicknesses. Objects to use for printing. Papers of different colours and textures. Collage materials such as fabrics, feathers, sequins, buttons, beads, magazine pictures, wallpaper pattern books. PVA glue and spreaders. Thick card for the collage figures or objects. Scissors.

What to do

1. Decide on the theme or characters to be included in the collage. As this is a group activity there need to be some large-scale characters or objects so that the children can discuss ideas and work co-operatively. In the *Fix it Duck* book there are four main characters: Duck, Sheep, Goat and Frog. There is also a bright red car and a leaky caravan to offer extra interest.

2. Decide with the children what the background will be together with the methods to be used in constructing the collage. Assist the children in sketching out the main parts of the collage together with any distinguishing features. Depending on the composition of the collage and the number of children in the group, it may be preferable to construct some of the characters separately and then put everything onto the background when all the work is completed.

3. Organisation of all of the collage materials is very important. Assist the children in organising the materials into predominant colours that will be used in this collage such as materials in different shades of yellow for *Fix it Duck*.

4. Work alongside the children supporting them with the techniques required in order to develop their ideas. Model the vocabulary used to describe textures and colours in addition to the materials chosen by the children.

5. Encourage the children to use a variety of techniques such as printing and painting in addition to collage techniques.

6. When all the work is completed assemble the collage, assisted by the children, and use the collage as a basis for discussion. Allow time for the children to appreciate their effort and success.

Extension activities

1. Using the same theme as for the collage, discuss with the children how they can further develop their ideas, but this time on an individual basis.

2. The children may decide to make a card, a calendar, a zigzag book, a mobile or a model. Encourage them to develop an innovative idea which they would not normally choose. This will enable them to develop their confidence and techniques, but remember that they may initially need more support.

3. Display the individual work in close proximity to the group collage together with the materials used for inspiration. If space allows, include in the display some photographs or the sketches of the work in progress, which will encourage the children to reflect on their work and to feel a sense of achievement.

4. Use the whole display as a resource for language learning enabling the children to recall and reflect on their contribution to the display.

Key vocabulary

Vocabulary linked to colour, textures and the collage materials. Vocabulary connected with the chosen book or painting or other inspirational materials. Positional vocabulary such as next to, near, underneath, on top of.

Links with the Foundation Stage for creative development

Begin to be interested in and describe the texture of things. Explore colours and begin to differentiate between colours. Begin to combine movement, materials, media or marks. Make constructions, collages, paintings, drawings and dances. Respond in a variety of ways to what they see, hear, smell, touch and feel.

Sensory play

 Activity name: Let's investigate!

Objectives

To enable children to enjoy sensory play.

To encourage children to investigate properties of different materials.

To offer opportunities to express ideas connected with investigating the materials.

Materials and preparation

A wide range of materials that can be used for sensory investigation particularly with regard to touch such as cooked spaghetti, play dough, cornflour, jelly, porridge, bubbles, water, dry and wet sand, leaves, pine cones, conkers and acorns. Large container for the material.

What to do

1. Decide which materials will be available for the children to investigate. On some occasions it is best to have one material available so that staff can work alongside the children as they play and model linked vocabulary and ask open-ended questions to extend the children's thinking. There is often the opportunity to introduce opposite words such as wet and dry or smooth and rough.

2. On other occasions the materials could be linked to a theme such as autumn when the leaves, pine cones and acorns would be accessible to the children.

3. The children can investigate what happens when water is added to some of the materials such as dry sand and dry cornflour.

4. The children need to have plenty of time to investigate the properties of the materials, enjoying their feel and possibly their smell. Some children will be initially reluctant to put their hands into the materials. Their feelings need to be respected and although the children can be encouraged, they may prefer to watch until they feel ready to join in. Remind the children to wash their hands thoroughly after playing with the materials, particularly when playing with the leaves and other natural materials.

5. Sensory play is often a calming experience for some children and play with water and dry sand can be a useful activity for children who need support and calm reassurance.

Extension activities

1. Carefully observe the children and listen to their comments connected with their play and the materials they are using. Extend the children's play and encourage them to develop their thinking by adding new toys to the sensory

materials, such as floating and sinking equipment to water play or adding cars and trucks to the wet sand which then could be used to form roads, tracks and tunnels.

2. Another way of developing the children's play is to use the materials for a range of creative activities or to further develop their interest through reading associated stories and factual books. The children who have enjoyed playing with the leaves may wish to find out more about the names of the leaves and the tree on which they grow. In this way the activities become child-led and of real interest to the children.

Key vocabulary
Vocabulary associated with the name of the materials and their feel such as soft, hard, wet, dry, smooth, rough, shiny and slippery.

Links with the Early Years Foundation Stage for creative development
Begin to be interested in and describe the texture of things. Experiment to create different textures. Respond in a variety of ways to what they see, hear, smell, touch and feel. Create constructions, collages, paintings and drawings.

Summary: key principles for promoting creative development

■ It is important to remember that not all creative activities have an 'end product'.

■ Children's creative development can best be promoted through supporting the children to develop their own ideas and in the way that they would prefer.

■ Creativity needs time to develop within a supportive and encouraging environment.

■ Creative activities are an important way for children to communicate and express their ideas, especially when their English language skills are still developing.

Resources

Practitioners can use the following children's books as indicated in the various chapters or adapt them to meet the needs of individual children.

A Carp for Kimiko. Virginia Kroll. Charlesbridge Publishing. 1996.

A Dark, Dark Tale. Ruth Brown. Translated into Chinese. Sylvia Denham. Mantra Lingua. 1998.

All Kinds of Feelings. Emma Brownjohn. Tango. 2003.

Best friends, Special friends. Susan Rollings. Orchard Books. ISBN 1–84121–156–7 2002.

Does a kangaroo have a mother too? Eric Carle. Collins. 2000.

Fix it Duck. Jez Alborough. HarperCollins. 2002.

Handa's Hen. Eileen Browne. Translated into Hindi by Awadesh Misra. Mantra Lingua. 2003.

Hippety-hop, Hippety hay. Opal Dunn. Frances Lincoln Limited. 1999.

If you're happy and you know it! Jan Ormerod. Oxford University Press. 2003.

I won't bite. Rod Campbell. Translated by Haans Associates. Roy Yates. 1996.

Jill and the Beanstalk. Manju Gregory. Translated into Polish by Sophie Bac. Mantra Lingua. 2004.

Let's look at families. Barbara Hunter. Heinemann. 2003.

Pocket Dogs. Margaret Wild. Scholastic Press. 2003.

Rainbow Fish. Marcus Pfister. North–South Books. 1998.

Room on the Broom. Julia Donaldson. Macmillan Children's Books. 2001.

Spot goes to School. Eric Hill. Puffin Books. 1998.

Tales from Acorn Wood – Postman Bear. Julia Donaldson. Macmillan Children's Books. 2003.

The Very Hungry Caterpillar. Eric Carle. Puffin Books. 1969.

The Wibbly, Wobbly Tooth. David Mills and Julia Growth. Mantra Lingua. 2002.

This Little Puffin. Elizabeth Matterson. Puffin Books. 1977.

Tom and Sofia start school. Henriette Barkow. Mantra Lingua. 2006.

When Grandma came. Jill Paton and Sophie Williams. Puffin Books. 1993.

Where does Thursday go? Janeen Brian. Southwood Books. 2002.

These professional texts offer more information on various early years topics:

Birth to Three Matters. DfES. 2003.

Care and Education of Young Bilinguals. Baker. Multilingual Matters. 2000.

Child Care and Education. Tina Bruce and Carolyn Meggitt. Hodder & Stoughton. 2005.

Child's Eye View of Festivals. Published by Child's Eye Media Ltd. (DVD/Video. n.d.)

Children in Action. Carmen Argondizzo. Prentice Hall. 1992.

Early Years Foundation Stage. DfES. 2007.

English as an Additional Language. Haslam, Wilkin, Kellet. David Fulton. 2005.

Foundation Stage Profile. QCA/DfES. 2003.

How to Make Observations and Assessments. Jackie Harding and Liz Meldon Smith. Hodder & Stoughton. 2005.

Language Displays. Moira Andrew. Scholastic Publications. 2000.

Learning Through Talk in the Early Years. Elizabeth Sharp. Paul Chapman Publishing. 2005.

Planning for Learning in the Foundation Stage. QCA/DfES. 2003.

Practice Guidance to the Early Years Foundation Stage Framework. DfES. 2007.

Principles into Practice. Blenkin and Kelly. Paul Chapman Publishing. 1997.

Promoting Learning for Bilingual Pupils 3–11. Edited by Jean Conteh. Paul Chapman Publishing. 2006.

Statutory Framework for the Early Years Foundation Stage. DfES. 2007.

Teaching Young Language Learners. AnnMaria Pinter. Oxford University Press. 2006.

Tell it Again. Gail Ellis and Jean Brewster. Penguin Books. 2002.

The Foundation Stage Teacher in Action. Margaret Edgington. Paul Chapman Publishing. 2004.

These websites provide a wealth of information relating to early years and bilingual education.

www.bfinclusion.org.uk – useful website giving commonly used words in different scripts including Russian, Japanese, Greek and Urdu.

www.blss.portsmouth.sch.uk – a wealth of ideas for first language and bilingual support.

www.childcarelink.gov.uk – for national and local information on childcare services.

www.dgteaz.org.uk – a website for Dingle, Granby, Toxteth and the City of Liverpool partnership containing resources to communicate with parents written in 32 languages including Chinese, Croatian and French.

www.direct.gov.uk – use to find information about a wide variety of early years matters.

www.everychildmatters.gov.uk – use to keep updated on all early years issues.

www.hitchams.suffolk.sch.uk – the website for Sir Robert Hitchams school with many ideas for the use of ICT.

www.inclusion.ngfl.gov.uk – resources for matters connected with teaching English as an additional language.

www.literacytrust.org.uk – many resources for supporting English as an additional language.

www.ltscotland.org.uk – the website for learning and teaching in Scotland providing an overview of research into bilingual language development in the early years.

www.mantralingua.com – look here for a wealth of multicultural resources including translations of books and story props.

www.naldic.org – the website for the National Association for Language Development in the Curriculum offering research evidence on early years provision and valuing children's home language.

www.ofsted.gov.uk – information of early years education and related matters.

www.parentscentre.gov.uk – a website in many different languages including Arabic, Chinese, Gujurati, Greek and Hindi with ideas for parents to help their children.

www.qca.org.uk – 'Language in common: assessing English as an additional language'.

www.ncsl.org.uk – the website for the National College for School Leadership providing information about applying for a place to study for the National Professional Qualification in Integrated Centre Leadership.

www.standards.dfes.gov.uk – research and development work to support bilingual learners.

www.surestart.gov.uk – an overview of services for children.

www.vangoghgallery.com – resources connected with Vincent Van Gogh and his sunflower paintings.

References

Andrew, M. (2000) *Language Displays*. Scholastic Publications: London.

Argondizzo, C. (1992) *Children in action*. Prentice Hall: London.

Baker, C. (2000) *Care and Education of Young Bilinguals*. Multilingual Matters: Clevedon.

Blenkin, G. and Kelly, A. V. *Principles into Practice*. Paul Chapman Publishing: London.

Bruce, T. and Meggitt, C. (2005) *Child Care and Education*. Hodder and Stoughton: London.

Child's Eye View of Festivals published by Child's Eye Media Ltd.

Clarke, P. (1999) *Supporting Bilingual Learners. Workshop Papers*. Free Kindergarten Association: Melbourne.

Conteh, J. (ed) (2006) *Promoting learning for Bilingual Pupils 3–11*. Paul Chapman Publishing: London.

DfES (2000) *Curriculum Guidance for the Foundation Stage*. DfES: London.

DfES/QCA (2003a) *Foundation Stage Profile*. DfES/QCA: London.

DfES/QCA (2003b) *Planning for Learning in the Foundation Stage*. DfES/QCA: London.

DfES (2003c) *Birth to Three Matters*. DfES: London.

DfES (2004) *Ten Year Strategy for Childcare: Choice for Parents, the Best Start for Children*. DfES: London.

DfES (2007) *The Early Years Foundation Stage*. DfES: London.

DfES (2007) *Statutory Framework for the Early Years*. DfES: London.

Edgington, M. (2004) *The Foundation Stage Teacher in Action*. Paul Chapman Publishing: London.

Ellis, G. and Brewster, J. (2002) *Tell it Again*. Penguin Books: London.

Foundation Stage Profile (2003) QCA/DfES.

Harding, J. and Meldon Smith, L. (2005) *How to make Observations and Assessments*. Hodder and Stoughton: London.

Haslam, L., Wilkin, Y. and Kellet, E. (2005) *English as an Additional Language*. David Fulton: London.

Parkee, P. and Drury, R. (2001) 'Language Development at Home and at School: Gains and losses in young bilinguals'. *Early Years*: 117–27.

Pinter, A. *Teaching Young Language Learners*. Oxford University Press.

Planning for Learning in the Foundation Stage. QCA/DfES.

Positively Pluringual (2005) Report from CiLT. The National Centre for Languages.

Sharp, E. (2005) *Learning Through Talk in the Early Years*. Paul Chapman Publishing: London.

Index

Promoting Learning for Bilingual Pupils 3-11
Opening Doors to Success

Edited by:
Jean Conteh, **University of Manchester**

'This book provides an excellent, practical guide on how to develop a bilingual approach in the classroom. In each chapter there are examples of practical, easy-to-implement strategies, which are firmly rooted in good EAL practice. Rather than suggesting that teachers have to adopt something that is additional or new, the idea is to build a bilingual approach into ongoing classroom activities and approaches, thereby promoting a sense of cultural belonging for all children' – *Janna Welsby, EAL Programme Consultant, Manchester Education Partnership*

Written by a team of teachers, this clear and accessible book shows readers how they can help bilingual learners in their classrooms to access the curriculum as effectively as possible.

Advice is included on:

- developing whole-school policies
- creating positive classroom settings to promote learning
- using drama
- supporting bilingual learners in the early years
- the importance of home-school links

There are also plenty of practical suggestions for ways to improve classroom practice, and some photocopiable material.

Contents
Introduction: Principles and Practices for Teaching Bilingual Learners/Promoting Positive Links between Home and School/Supporting Bilingual Learners in the Early Years/The Importance of Talk for Learning/Using a 'Bilingual Approach' to Promote Learning/Using Drama to Promote Learning. Promoting a Positive Whole-School Ethos/Rounding it Off

July 2006 • 128 pages
Hardcover (978-1-4129-2083-4) Price £60.00 • Paperback (978-1-4129-2084-1) Price £17.99

Paul Chapman Publishing
A SAGE Publications Company

Visit our website at
www.paulchapmanpublishing.co.uk
to order online and receive free postage and packaging

Developing Pre-School Communication and Language

Cd-Rom

Chris Dukes, **Area SENCOs, London**
Maggie Smith, **Area SENCOs, London**

Looking for advice on how to develop communication and language skills in the pre-school?

Packed with helpful advice on supporting and developing the crucial language and communication skills of the children in your early years setting, this book provides clear guidance on appropriate expectations for each age group between birth to five.

The book includes:

- advice on how to support language development in all children, including those with special educational needs
- practical ideas and strategies for practitioners and parents
- guidance on when to seek advice and working with other professionals
- activities and case studies
- a CD Rom with useful photocopiable resources.

This book is ideal for all those working with the 0 to 5 age range, such as pre-school practitioners, nursery managers, advisory teachers, SENCOs, Inclusion Officers and Child Care and Education students and tutors.
Chris Dukes and Maggie Smith are both Area SENCOs who work closely with pre-school SENCOs and Managers on a daily basis.

Contents
Getting Started: People, Places, Play and Planning/Babies 0-11 months/Babies and Toddlers 8-20 months/Toddlers 16-26 months/Toddlers and Children 22-36 months/Children 30-50 months/Children 40-60 months/Working with Young Bilingual Children/Creating Language Opportunities/Meeting Individual Needs

Oct 2007 • 128 pages
Hardcover (978-1-4129-4523-3) Price £60.00 • Paperback (978-1-4129- 4524-0) Price £18.99

Paul Chapman Publishing
A SAGE Publications Company

Visit our website at
www.paulchapmanpublishing.co.uk
to order online and receive free postage and packaging

Creative Activities for the Early Years

Stella Skinner

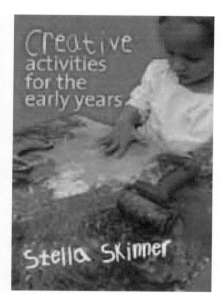

'Inspirational... This book is easy to read, refreshing and exciting, and I would recommend it to all those working with young children. It is also useful for students, clearly articulating the reasons for providing well-organised child-initiated creative opportunities rather than adult-directed activities' – **Nursery World**

'It is a book that celebrates and encourages original thought and action to support learning through exploration and investigation, recognising that creativity is about representing one's own image and not reproducing someone else's' – **Early Years Educator**

Packed full of exciting ideas and powerful visual aids, this book will help those working with young children to encourage and nurture their creativity and imagination. The book takes examples of what has worked in an early years setting, and transfers these inspirational activities onto the page.

The book includes:

– practical activities in Art, Dance and Music and ideas on how to link them together;
– advice on how to make the most of music, lighting, space and nursery resources;
– showing how the work supports the Foundation Stage Curriculum;
– ideas for cross-curricular work;
– suggestions for recording children's progress;
– advice on how to choose materials, and a list of specialist suppliers.

Everyone involved in working with young children should read this book. Nursery practitioners, early years teachers, Sure Start workers, play workers and Children's Centre staff will find it an invaluable resource. It is also useful for specialist staff in hospitals and other areas of health.

Contents
Introduction/Approach to Creative Learning in Early Years/Visual Arts/Music/Dance/Combined Arts/Curriculum Guidance/Materials and Suppliers/Further Reading and References

Feb 2007 • 120 pages
Hardcover (978-1-4129-3447-3) Price £60.00 • Paperback (978-1-4129-3448-0) Price £16.99

Paul Chapman Publishing

A SAGE Publications Company

Visit our website at
www.paulchapmanpublishing.co.uk
to order online and receive free postage and packaging